CREATIVE WINDOW TREATMENTS

Forty-Five Styles Shown Step-by-Step

The Home Decorating Institute™

Copyright © 1992 Cy DeCosse Incorporated 5900 Green Oak Drive Minnetonka, Minnesota 55343
1-800-328-3895 All rights reserved Printed in U.S.A.

Library of Congress Cataloging-in-Publication Data Creative window treatments. p. cm. — (Arts & crafts for home decorating)
Includes index. ISBN 0-86573-352-X ISBN-0-86573-355-4 (pbk.)   1. Drapery. 2. Windows in interior decoration. I. Cy DeCosse
Incorporated. II. Series.   TT390.C74 1992 747' .3—dc20   91-42084

CONTENTS

Basic Window Treatments

Designer Window Treatments

Top Treatments & Accessories

Alternative Window Treatments

SELECTING A STYLE

Window treatments are an integral part of a decorating scheme. Windows that are beautifully dressed enrich the style of a room. Some provide a subtle backdrop for other elements in the room, while others are the focal point. From breezy, open-weave curtains to layered draperies and top treatments, the choices for window treatments are endless.

In addition to enhancing the decorating scheme, window treatments serve several purposes. A window treatment can filter sunlight during the day and close out the nighttime darkness. It can allow fresh air to circulate into the room or provide weather and noise insulation. A window treatment can frame a magnificent view or obscure a view and offer privacy. It can also emphasize architectural details or add visual width and height to a window.

When you are deciding on the type of window treatment to use, consider the style of the window. Some window treatments may not be suitable for the type of window you have. Some windows slide up and down, some slide sideways, and still others swing in or out. If you want to open and close the windows for air, select window treatments that will not get in the way. If you have casement windows, the window treatment must not interfere with the protruding handles that operate the windows.

Some windows need little or no window treatment. Add shutters to complement the woodwork, or if the view is beautiful and privacy is assured, consider etching a corner of the glass and setting a plant on the window sill to accent the view.

The fabrics and hardware you select affect how formal or informal the window treatment is. For example, a swag made from tapestry and draped over a highly polished pole is elegant and formal, while a cotton swag with a wood pole and shutters has a casual, informal look. Sheers and other unlined treatments are more light and airy than those that are lined. However, lining adds extra body, giving a more custom look as well as insulating qualities.

STYLES OF WINDOW TREATMENTS

Double-hung window.

Double-hung and casement windows are the most common types of windows used in houses. The choice of window treatments, or combinations of treatments, is virtually unlimited for dressing these types of windows. To keep windows operational, select window treatments that do not interfere with raising and lowering double-hung windows or cranking open casement windows.

Casement window.

Relaxed Roman shade and valance (page 56).

Fabric-covered cornice (page 91) and pleated shade.

Tapered valance (page 82) and pleated shade.

Curtain from sheets (page 67).

Tieback curtains from sheets (page 67).

Tapered valance (page 82) and shutters with inserts (page 117).

*Lace cloud shade
(page 62).*

*Arched rod-pocket valance (page 81)
and painted shutters (page 117).*

*Relaxed Roman shade (page 56)
and fabric-covered cornice with
molding (page 91).*

*Swag (page 73) and painted shutters
(page 117).*

*Rod-pocket curtains (page 25) and
valance from lace tablecloth (page 87).*

*Draperies with goblet pleats
(page 45).*

*Tie-tab curtains
(page 51).*

*Swag with knotted jabots
(page 77).*

*Self-styling curtains
(page 32).*

Shelf above window (page 114).

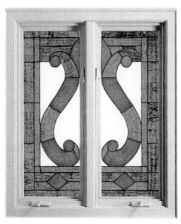

Faux stained glass (page 118).

Valance from tablecloth (page 86).

Knotted rod-pocket curtain panel (page 29).

Tie-tab curtains (page 51) and valance (page 81).

Rod-pocket curtains (page 25) and tiebacks (page 102).

Draperies with double pinch pleats (page 44).

Ruffled tapered valance (page 84).

Self-styling curtains (page 32).

*Vent hose cornice (page 97) and
pleated shades.*

*Etched glass
(page 123).*

*Rod-pocket curtains (page 25) and
floral top treatment (page 99).*

*Swag (page 73) with fabric-covered
pole and ball finials
(page 106).*

*Knotted rod-pocket curtain
(page 29) and wallpapered cornice
(page 95).*

*Rod-pocket curtain (page 25) with
garland tieback
(page 103).*

*Swag with towel rings
(page 76).*

*Glass shelves (page 114) and cafe
curtains (page 28).*

*Swag (page 73) with rod-pocket
curtains (page 25).*

STYLES FOR SPECIALTY WINDOWS

Some windows require special window treatments. For a window that is unique in styling or shape, select a treatment, such as etched glass, that enhances the window without covering it up. For multiple windows, a single window treatment can unify the windows. For windows on patio doors, the window treatment should not interfere with operating the doors.

Awning window can be embellished with faux stained glass (page 118), which offers some privacy.

Multiple windows unified with pleated draperies (page 37) have a traditional, sophisticated look.

Double window is unified by a swag (page 73) that offers unrestricted light and view. The cafe curtains (page 28) add privacy.

Kitchen window has a casual look with kitchen towel curtains (page 69).

Awning window is enhanced with etched glass (page 123).

Bay window is framed at the top with a rod-pocket valance (page 80); the accompanying cafe curtains (page 28) are easily installed into the bay with tension rods.

Arched French door *is customized with an elegant design in etched glass (page 123).*

Sliding patio door *features a floral top treatment (page 98) to bring the look of the garden indoors. The pleated shade raises out of the way when the door is being used.*

Patio door *is covered with shutters (page 117), which slide open to clear the door opening.*

Bay window *is highlighted with smocked tieback curtains (page 32), which fit within the bay.*

Corner windows *are unified by draping them with self-styling curtains (page 32).*

HARDWARE NEEDS

The hardware you select can be decorative as well as functional. For elaborate window treatments, traditional poles with detailed finials are available, as well as decorative tieback holders. And sleek, contemporary hardware is available for a more understated look. For a creative, nontraditional look, consider using decorative towel rings (page 76), vent hoses (page 97), or other items as hardware.

Select the type of hardware you want before measuring for a window treatment. The cut length of drapery panels will vary, depending on the hardware used.

CURTAIN RODS

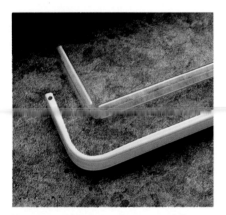

Narrow curtain rods are used for rod-pocket window treatments. When sheer fabric is used, select a rod of clear or translucent plastic that will not show through the fabric.

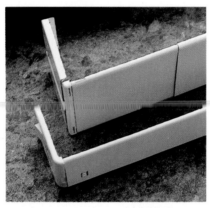

Wide curtain rods are available in both 2½" (6.5 cm) and 4½" (11.5 cm) widths. They add depth and interest to rod-pocket window treatments. Corner connectors make these rods suitable for bay and corner windows.

Tension rods, used inside window frames for cafe curtains and valances, are held in place by the pressure of a spring inside the rod. Because mounting brackets are not used, the woodwork is not damaged by screws.

Sash rods use shallow mounting brackets so the window treatment hangs close to the glass. Available flat or round, they are commonly used for stretched curtains on doors.

Cafe rods are used with or without rings. Available in several finishes, including brass and enamel, they are used for hand-drawn window treatments, such as tie-tab curtains.

Hand-draw wood pole sets with rings are available in several finishes or unfinished. The poles may be used with finials or elbows.

TRAVERSE DRAPERY RODS

Conventional traverse rods are available in white, ivory, and wood tones.

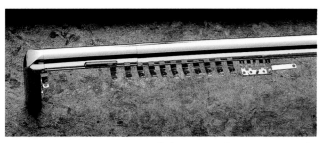

Contemporary traverse rods have metallic and pearlized finishes in several colors.

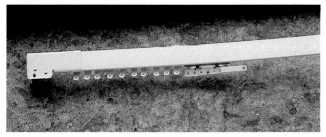

Brass traverse pole sets, with or without rings, come with various finial styles. The poles are plain or fluted.

Wood traverse pole sets with rings are available in several finishes.

Flexible traverse rods are used for pleated draperies on bay windows. A single flexible rod is easily installed into a bay opening.

Marbleized traverse pole sets, available in white or black, have a sculptured, classic look.

HARDWARE ACCESSORIES

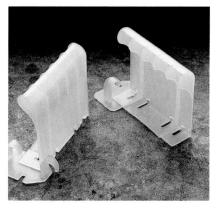

Concealed tieback holders fit behind the last fold of pleated or rod-pocket draperies to prevent the tieback from crushing the draperies. The projection is adjustable.

Decorative tieback holders are used instead of fabric tiebacks to hold draperies in place. They may also be used for swag window treatments.

Swag holders support the draped fabric in swag window treatments.

INSTALLING HARDWARE

Support drapery rods with center brackets to prevent them from bowing. The brackets are usually positioned at intervals of 45" (115 cm) or less, across the width of the rod. Whenever possible, screw the brackets into wall studs. If it is necessary to position brackets between wall studs into drywall or plaster, use molly bolts for installing hardware that will support heavy window treatments. For supporting lightweight window treatments or for installing tieback holders, plastic anchors may be used instead of molly bolts.

HOW TO INSTALL A ROD BRACKET USING MOLLY BOLTS

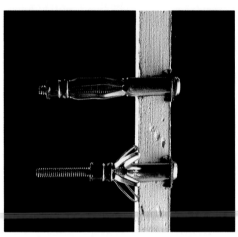

1 Hold drapery rod bracket at desired placement. Mark screw locations. Drill holes for molly bolts into drywall or plaster; drill bit diameter depends on size of molly bolt. For heavy window treatments, two molly bolts may be used for each bracket.

2 Tap molly bolt into drilled hole, using hammer. Tighten screw; molly bolt expands, preventing it from pulling out of the wall.

3 Remove screw from molly bolt; insert screw into rod bracket. Align the screw with installed molly bolt. Screw the bracket securely in place.

HOW TO INSTALL A TIEBACK HOLDER USING PLASTIC ANCHORS

1 Hold tieback holder at desired height for tiebacks; position tieback holder below end bracket of drapery rod so drapery will hang straight at sides. Mark screw locations.

2 Drill holes for plastic anchors into drywall or plaster. Use two plastic anchors for each tieback holder. Tap plastic anchors into drilled holes, using hammer.

3 Insert screw into tieback holder. Align screw with installed plastic anchor. Screw tieback holder securely in place.

HOW TO INSTALL A TRAVERSE ROD

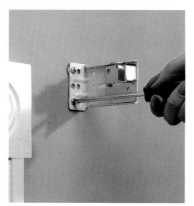

1 Mount the end rod brackets (opposite) with U-shaped socket facing upward.

2 Hook lipped support clip of center bracket over center of rod; position rod, fitting ends of rod into end brackets. Mark screw holes for center bracket.

3 Take rod down, and mount center bracket. Lift the rod into position again; snap center support clip over rod, hooking it into groove at front of rod. Using screwdriver, turn metal cam on underside of support clip counterclockwise, locking clip in place.

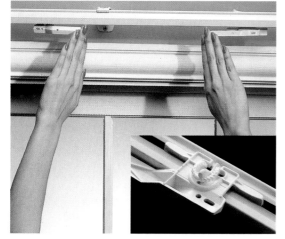

4 Push overlap and underlap master slides to opposite ends of rod. At left side, reach behind underlap slide for the cord. Pull cord slightly to form small loop; hook loop securely over plastic finger that projects from the back of master slide (inset).

5 Separate the stem from pulley base; hold base against wall near the floor, directly below a point 2" (5 cm) in from the right end bracket of rod. Mark screw locations; mount bracket.

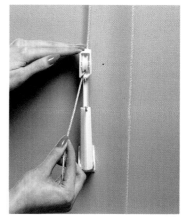

6 Attach stem to pulley base. Pull up on cord housing, exposing hole on inner stem. Insert small nail through hole so stem remains extended. Attach cord to pulley, slipping loop end of cord through slot in cord housing.

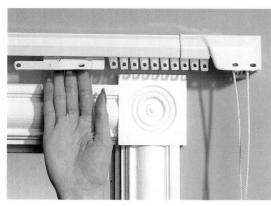

7 Reach behind overlap master slide at right end of rod; locate two knots at back of slide.

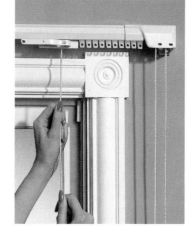

8 Pull the knot nearest the glides until cord hanging at side of rod is taut against pulley wheel. Tie a new knot in cord at back of slide, with excess cord hanging down. Remove nail from inner stem of pulley. Cut off excess cord; tighten knot securely.

INSTALLING MOUNTING BOARDS

When window treatments are mounted on boards instead of hung on drapery rods, cover the mounting board with fabric for a professional look.

The mounting board may be installed inside or outside the window frame. For an inside mount, the board is screwed into the top of the window frame.

For an outside mount, the mounting board is installed at the top of the window frame or on the wall above the window. For clearance, the board is cut longer than the width of the frame or undertreatment and projects out from the wall farther than the frame or undertreatment

Angle irons are used to install an outside-mounted board. The angle irons must be a little shorter than the width of the mounting board. Whenever possible, screw the angle irons into wall studs, using pan-head screws. If it is necessary to install angle irons between wall studs into drywall or plaster, use molly bolts to ensure a secure installation.

HOW TO COVER THE MOUNTING BOARD

CUTTING DIRECTIONS

Cut the fabric to cover the mounting board, with the width of the fabric equal to the distance around the board plus 1" (2.5 cm) and the length of the fabric equal to the length of the board plus 4½" (11.5 cm).

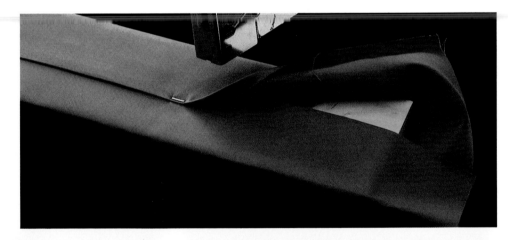

1 Center board on wrong side of fabric. Staple one long edge of fabric to board, placing staples about 8" (20.5 cm) apart; do not staple within 6" (15 cm) of ends. Wrap fabric around board. Fold under ⅜" (1 cm) on long edge; staple to board, placing staples about 6" (15 cm) apart.

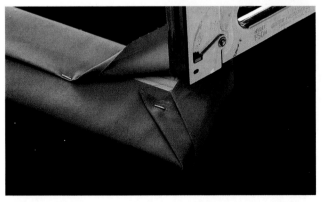

2 Miter fabric at corners on side of board with unfolded fabric edge; finger-press. Staple miters in place near raw edge.

3 Miter fabric at corners on side of board with folded fabric edge; finger-press. Fold under excess fabric at ends; staple near fold.

HOW TO INSTALL AN INSIDE-MOUNTED BOARD

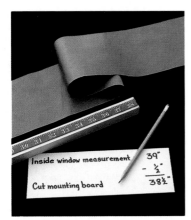

1 Cut 1 × 1 mounting board ½" (1.3 cm) shorter than inside measurement of window frame. This ensures that mounting board will fit inside the frame after it is covered with fabric.

2 Cover mounting board (opposite). From the bottom of board, predrill screw holes through board and into window frame, using ⅛" (3.18 mm) drill bit; drill holes ¾" (2 cm) from each end of board and in center for wide window treatments.

3 Staple window treatment to mounting board. Secure board, using 8 × 1½" (3.8 cm) pan-head screws.

HOW TO INSTALL AN OUTSIDE-MOUNTED BOARD

1 Cut mounting board 2" (5 cm) longer than width of undertreatment or window frame. If the outside-mounted window treatment is used alone, a 1 × 2 mounting board may be used. If the outside-mounted treatment is used over an undertreatment, the mounting board should be at least 2" (5 cm) wider than the projection of the undertreatment.

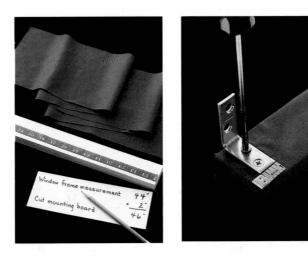

2 Cover board (opposite). Mark screw holes for angle irons on bottom of board, positioning angle irons within 1" (2.5 cm) of each end of board and at 45" (115 cm) intervals or less. Predrill screw holes into board; size of drill bit depends on screw size required for angle iron. Screw angle irons onto board.

3 Hold board at desired placement, making sure it is level; mark screw holes on wall or window frame.

4 Remove angle irons from board. Secure angle irons to wall, using molly bolts (page 14) or ¾" (2 cm) pan-head screws.

5 Staple window treatment to the mounting board. Place mounting board on installed angle irons. Screw angle irons onto board

MEASURING THE WINDOW

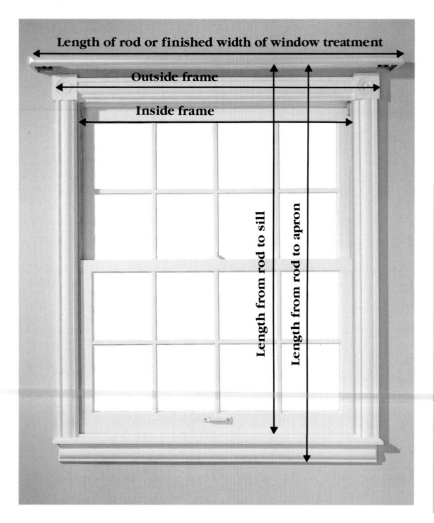

Length of rod or finished width of window treatment

Outside frame

Inside frame

Length from rod to sill

Length from rod to apron

TIPS FOR MEASURING

Allow ½" (1.3 cm) clearance between the bottom of the drapery and the floor when measuring for floor-length draperies. For loosely woven fabrics, allow 1" (2.5 cm) clearance.

Allow 4" to 6" (10 to 15 cm) clearance above baseboard heaters for safety.

Measure for all draperies in the room to the same height from the floor for a uniform look. Use the highest window in the room as the standard for measuring for the treatments on the other windows.

Make underdraperies ½" (1.3 cm) shorter than the overdraperies at the top and bottom, so they will not show above or below the overdraperies.

After selecting the window treatment, install the hardware and take the necessary measurements. For accurate measurements, use a folding ruler or metal tape measure. Measure and record the measurements for each window separately, even if the windows appear to be the same size.

Depending on the style of window treatment, rods and mounting boards may be mounted inside or outside the window frame. For an inside mount, install the hardware inside the top of the frame so the molding is exposed. For an outside mount, install the hardware at the top of the window frame or on the wall above the window. When the hardware is mounted above the window frame, visual height is added to the window.

Some window treatments can be mounted so they cover part of the wall at the sides of the window, adding visual width. When window treatments are mounted onto the wall, more glass can be exposed, letting in more light.

You will need to determine the finished length and finished width of the window treatment. Then determine the cut length and cut width by adding the amounts needed for hems, rod pockets, seams, and fullness. If a patterned fabric is used, you will also need to allow extra fabric for matching the pattern (page 20).

To determine the finished length of the window treatment, measure from the rod or the mounting board to where you want the lower edge of the window treatment. The measurement is usually taken from the top of the rod or board. When decorative rods are used, the measurement is taken from the pin hole in one of the rings or gliders. Depending on the style of the treatment, you may need to add to this measurement an amount for heading or clearance above the rod. Specific instructions for determining the finished length are included in the cutting directions for each window treatment in this book.

To determine the finished width of the window treatment, measure the length of the drapery rod or mounting board. For some treatments, it may also be necessary to measure the width of the return (opposite).

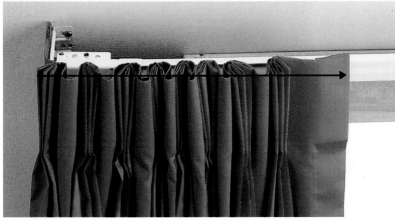

Stacking space is the distance from the sides of the window to the brackets, that allows draperies on traverse rods to clear, or partially clear, the window when the draperies are drawn open; this is sometimes referred to as *stackback*. Stationary window treatments may also be mounted so they "stack" at the sides of the window.

Overlap is the area where the drapery panels lap over each other at the center of a two-way traverse rod. The standard overlap is 3½" (9 cm).

Projection is the distance the rod or mounting board stands out from the wall.

Return is the portion of the drapery extending from the corner of the rod to the wall, enclosing the brackets of the drapery hardware. For draperies mounted on traverse rods, the return is ½" (1.3 cm) more than the projection of the rod.

Fullness of window treatments can vary, depending on the look desired. It is referred to as two, two and one-half, or three times fullness; for example, two times fullness means that the width of the window treatment measures two times the width of the rod or mounting board. For mediumweight to heavyweight fabrics, use two to two and one-half times fullness (left). For sheer and lightweight fabrics, use two and one-half to three times fullness (right).

CUTTING & SEAMING FABRIC

Many window treatments are made from fabric yardage. After taking the necessary measurements and determining the finished size of the window treatment, you will be able to estimate how much fabric you need.

To determine the cut length and cut width of a fabric that does not require matching, add the amounts needed for any hems, rod pockets, headings, ease, seam allowances, and fullness to the finished size of the window treatment. For example, if you are sewing a rod-pocket curtain, add the amount needed for rod pockets, headings, and hems to the finished length; then add side hems, seam allowances, and fullness to the finished width. Each window treatment in this book includes the instructions for determining the cut length and width of the fabric. For patterned fabrics, allow extra yardage.

Often a window treatment requires more than one width of fabric. To determine the number of widths needed, divide the calculated cut width of the window treatment by the width of the fabric. To calculate the amount of fabric you will need, multiply the cut length of the window treatment by the number of fabric widths needed; this is the total fabric length in inches (centimeters). Divide this measurement by 36" (100 cm) to determine the number of yards (meters) required.

Cut the number of fabric widths you need to the calculated cut length, by marking the fabric at a right angle to the selvage and cutting on the marked line; then seam the widths together. If you are sewing a pair of drapery panels, seam one-half the total widths together for each panel. If the number of widths is an odd number, divide one of the widths in half lengthwise, using one half for each panel.

PATTERNED FABRICS

Extra yardage is usually required for matching patterned fabrics at the seamlines. Measure the pattern repeat of the fabric; this is the lengthwise distance from one point on the pattern, such as the tip of a leaf, to the same point in the next pattern design. Add the amounts needed for hems, rod pockets, headings, ease, seam allowances, and fullness to the finished length, to determine how long the lengths of fabric need to be. Then round this measurement up to the next number divisible by the size of the pattern repeat to determine the cut length.

For example, if the pattern repeat is 24" (61 cm), and the finished length plus hems, rod pockets, and other allowances is 45" (115 cm), the actual cut length is 48" (122 cm). To have patterns match from one panel to the next, cut each length of fabric at the same point on the pattern repeat.

Calculate the amount of fabric you will need, adding one additional pattern repeat so you can adjust the placement of the pattern on the cut lengths. Seam the fabric widths together with the patterns matching. Then trim the panels to the exact length required for the window treatment.

TYPES OF SEAMS

Straight-stitch seam, sewn on the conventional sewing machine, is pressed open for a smooth, flat seam. The selvages are trimmed away either before or after seaming the fabric. For lined window treatments, it is not necessary to finish the seam allowances.

4-thread or 5-thread overlock seam, stitched on a serger, is self-finished and does not stretch out of shape. Press the seam allowances to one side.

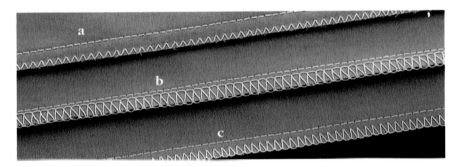

Combination seams are stitched using the straight stitch on the conventional machine. The seam allowances are trimmed to 1/4" (6 mm), trimming away the selvages, and finished using the zigzag stitch **(a)** on a conventional machine or a 3-thread **(b)** or 2-thread **(c)** overlock stitch on a serger. Press the seam allowances to one side.

MATCHING A PATTERNED FABRIC

1 Position fabric widths, right sides together, matching the selvages. Fold back the upper selvage until pattern matches; lightly press foldline.

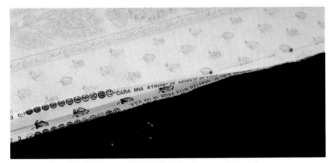

2 Unfold selvage, and pin fabric widths together on foldline. Check the match from right side.

3 Repin fabric so pins are perpendicular to foldline; stitch on foldline, using straight stitch. Trim fabric to finished length plus hems, rod pockets, and other allowances, as calculated opposite.

Basic Window
Treatments

ROD-POCKET CURTAINS

Rod-pocket curtains are simply flat panels of fabric with stitched-in headings, rod pockets, and double-fold hems. The style can be varied by changing the size of the heading, the length of the treatment, and how the fabric is draped (pages 28 and 29). Use a 1", 2½", or 4½" (2.5, 6.5, or 11.5 cm) curtain rod or a drapery pole set, depending on the look you prefer. Trims may be stitched along the inner edge of the finished curtain panels for a decorative effect, as shown opposite.

The curtains may be either unlined or lined. Sheers and other unlined curtains are more light and airy than curtains that are lined. However, lining adds extra body to curtains, giving them the look and drape of custom window treatments. The lining extends into the heading to keep the ruffled edge from drooping and extends into the side hems for firmer edges that hang well.

Before you sew, decide where you want the window treatment to be, and install the rod. Measure from the bottom of the rod to where you want the lower edge of the curtain. To determine the finished length, add the desired heading depth and the depth of the rod pocket. This is what the curtain will measure from the top of the heading to the hemmed lower edge.

MATERIALS

- Decorator fabric.
- Lining fabric, if desired.
- Curtain rod or pole set.
- Drapery weights.

CUTTING DIRECTIONS

Determine the depth of the rod pocket and heading (below) and the width of the hem at the lower edge. A 4" (10 cm) double-fold hem is often used for the decorator fabric; if the curtain is lined, a 2" (5 cm) double-fold hem is used for the lining.

The cut length of the decorator fabric is equal to the desired finished length of the curtain plus the depth of the heading and the rod pocket, ½" (1.3 cm) for turn-under at the upper edge, and twice the width of the hem.

The cut width of the decorator fabric is determined by the width of the curtain rod and the amount of fullness desired in the curtain. For sheer fabrics, allow two and one-half to three times the width of the rod for fullness; for heavier fabrics, allow two to two and one-half times. After multiplying the width of the rod times the desired fullness, add 6" (15 cm) for each panel to allow for 1½" (3.8 cm) double-fold side hems. If it is necessary to piece fabric widths together to make each panel, also add 1" (2.5 cm) for each seam.

The cut length of the lining is 5" (12.5 cm) shorter than the cut length of the decorator fabric; this allows for a 2" (5 cm) double-fold hem at the lower edge and for the lining to be 1" (2.5 cm) shorter than the curtain when it is finished. The cut width of the lining is equal to the cut width of the decorator fabric.

TERMS TO KNOW

Heading (a) is the portion at the top of a rod-pocket curtain that forms a ruffle when the curtain is on the rod. The width of the heading is the distance from the top of the finished curtain to the top stitching line of the rod pocket.

Rod pocket (b) is the portion of the curtain where the curtain rod is inserted; stitching lines at the top and bottom of the rod pocket keep the rod in place. To determine the depth of the rod pocket, measure around the widest part of the rod or pole; add ½" (1.3 cm) ease to this measurement, and divide by two.

HOW TO SEW UNLINED ROD-POCKET CURTAINS

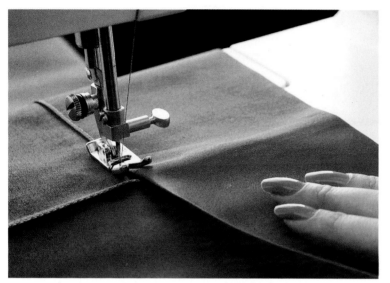

1 Seam fabric widths, if necessary, for each curtain panel. At lower edge, press under 4" (10 cm) twice to wrong side; stitch to make double-fold hem, using straight stitch or blindstitch.

2 Press under 1½" (3.8 cm) twice on sides. Tack drapery weights inside the side hems, about 3" (7.5 cm) from lower edge. Stitch to make double-fold hems.

3 Press under ½" (1.3 cm) on upper edge. Then press under an amount equal to rod-pocket depth plus heading depth. Stitch close to first fold.

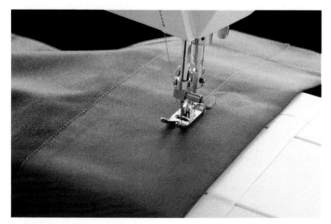

4 Stitch again at depth of heading, using tape on bed of machine as stitching guide.

5 Insert pole or rod through rod pocket, gathering fabric evenly. Install pole on brackets.

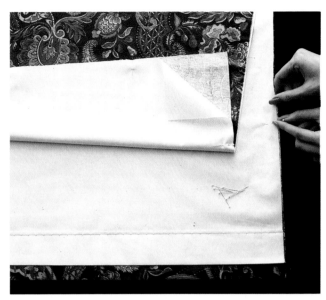

1 Seam decorator fabric widths, if necessary, for each curtain panel; repeat for lining panel. At lower edge of curtain panel, press under 4" (10 cm) twice to wrong side; stitch to make double-fold hem. Repeat for hem on lining panel, pressing under 2" (5 cm) twice.

2 Place curtain panel and lining panel wrong sides together, matching raw edges at sides and upper edge; pin. At the bottom, the lining panel will be 1" (2.5 cm) shorter than curtain panel.

4 Press and stitch rod pocket and heading as in steps 3 and 4, opposite; lining and curtain panels are folded as one fabric.

3 Press under 1½" (3.8 cm) twice on sides, folding lining and curtain panel as one fabric. Tack drapery weights inside the side hems, about 3" (7.5 cm) from lower edge. Stitch to make double-fold hems, using blindstitch or straight stitch.

5 Insert pole or rod through rod pocket, gathering fabric evenly. Install pole on brackets.

ROD-POCKET CURTAIN VARIATIONS

Curtains with contrasting edging (page 30) are easy to sew, with just one extra seam at the top of the curtain. The contrasting trim may be used to emphasize one of the colors in a patterned fabric.

Cafe curtains are a shorter version of basic rod-pocket curtains (page 25). These sheer curtains allow sunlight to come into the room.

Stretched rod-pocket curtains (page 31), made from sheer fabric, softly filter the light through the windows on doors. Because the panels are stretched between two rods, the fullness is controlled.

Knotted rod-pocket curtains (page 31) are informal and unstructured. Made from luxurious lightweight fabric, the knotted curtains have soft, appealing folds.

HOW TO SEW CURTAINS WITH CONTRASTING EDGING

MATERIALS

• Decorator fabrics in two colors.
• Lining fabric, if desired.
• Curtain rod or pole set.
• Drapery weights.

CUTTING DIRECTIONS

Determine the depth of the rod pocket and heading and the width of the hem at the lower edge (page 25).

The cut length of each curtain panel is equal to the desired finished length of the curtain plus twice the width of the hem. Determine the cut width of each curtain panel as for the basic curtain on page 25.

Cut one contrasting piece for each curtain panel, to the same width as the panel. Contrasting pieces should be equal to twice the desired width of the trim plus the depth of the heading and the rod pocket plus ½" (1.3 cm) turn-under at the upper edge.

If lining is desired, the cut length of the lining is equal to the desired finished length of the curtain plus the depth of the heading and the rod pocket plus 3½" (9 cm). This allows for ½" (1.3 cm) turn-under at the upper edge, 4" (10 cm) for 2" (5 cm) double-fold hem at the lower edge, and for the lining to be 1" (2.5 cm) shorter than the curtain when it is finished.

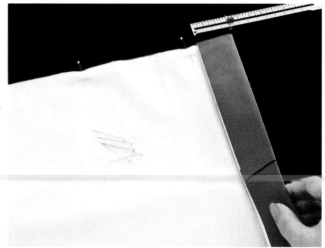

1 Seam fabric widths and stitch hems at lower edge of panels as on page 27, step 1; lining may be omitted. Stitch contrasting piece to upper edge of curtain panel, right sides together, with stitching a distance from raw edge equal to desired finished width of trim.

2 Press seam allowances toward contrasting piece. Pin lining to curtain panel as on page 27, step 2. Press under 1½" (3.8 cm) twice on sides, folding lining and curtain panels together as one; tack drapery weights inside the side hems, about 3" (7.5 cm) from lower edge. Stitch to make double-fold hems, using straight stitch or blindstitch.

3 Press under ½" (1.3 cm) on upper edge of contrasting piece and lining. Then press contrasting piece and lining to wrong side of curtain, with contrasting edging of desired width showing on right side. Stitch close to first fold. Stitch again at depth of heading, using tape on bed of machine as stitching guide. Insert curtain rod or pole through rod pocket, gathering fabric evenly. Install rod on brackets.

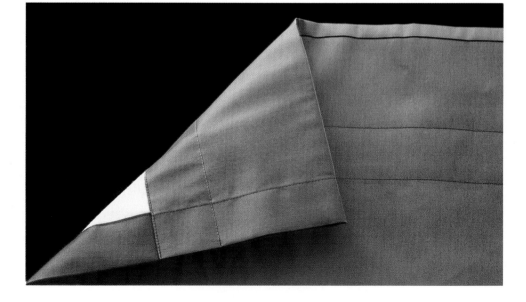

HOW TO SEW STRETCHED ROD-POCKET CURTAINS

MATERIALS

- Sheer decorator fabric.
- Two curtain rods or sash rods.

CUTTING DIRECTIONS

Determine the depth of the rod pockets and headings (page 25) at the top and bottom of the curtain.

To determine the cut length of the curtain panel, measure from the bottom of the top rod to the top of the bottom rod; then add four times the desired heading depth and four times the rod-pocket depth plus 1" (2.5 cm) for turning under the edges. Also add ½" (1.3 cm) ease; this is necessary for gathering the curtain on the rod. Determine the cut width of the curtain panel as for the basic curtain on page 25.

1 Seam fabric widths, if necessary. Press under 1½" (3.8 cm) twice on sides of curtain panel; stitch to make double-fold hems, using straight stitch or blindstitch.

2 Press and stitch rod pockets and headings at upper and lower edges as on page 26, steps 3 and 4. Insert curtain rods through rod pockets, gathering fabric evenly. Install rods on brackets.

HOW TO SEW KNOTTED ROD-POCKET CURTAINS

MATERIALS

- Sheer or lightweight decorator fabric.
- Curtain rod.
- One tenter hook or cup hook and one pin-on tieback ring for each curtain panel; drapery weights.

CUTTING DIRECTIONS

This treatment is suitable for unlined curtain panels for a rod width up to 36" (91.5 cm). Cut the fabric as for rod-pocket curtains (page 25), allowing an extra 20" to 25" (51 to 63.5 cm) of length for tying the knot.

1 Make unlined curtain (page 26). Insert curtain rod through rod pocket, gathering fabric evenly. Install rod on brackets. Tie curtain panel into a knot at desired location, arranging fabric for a pleasing look.

2 Attach tenter hook or cup hook to wall behind knot. Attach pin-on tieback ring to knot on wrong side of curtain panel. Secure curtain panel to hook on wall.

SELF-STYLING CURTAINS

Smocking tape *makes neatly smocked folds at the heading. For this bay window, two panels are held neatly in place with tiebacks.*

Shirring tape *creates a softly gathered heading that is consistent with the flowing fabric draped softly over a decorator pole.*

Self-styling curtains *are gathered by pulling the woven-in cords on the tape (opposite). Three styles are shown.*

Curtains can be sewn quickly and easily, using self-styling tapes. The tape is applied flat to the top of the curtain panels, and the woven-in cords are pulled to create the heading of the curtain. For best results, use self-styling tapes on mediumweight to lightweight fabrics.

Self-styling tapes are available in various widths and styles. You may choose either sew-in or fusible tapes. Sew-in tapes are the most versatile, because they can be used for either lined or unlined curtains. Fusible tapes, however, work well for extra-quick, unlined curtains. On some fabrics, the fusible adhesive may affect the appearance of the curtain on the right side; test a piece of the fusible tape on the fabric you have selected before sewing the curtains.

Because most self-styling tapes form rather stiff headings, they are usually used for stationary window treatments. The curtains may be installed on standard or decorative curtain rods or on pole sets with rings. To hang panels from flat curtain rods, use drapery pins. Some tapes have loops woven into them for securing the drapery pins, and some manufacturers provide special pins for installation.

The amount of fullness needed in the curtain depends on the style of tape you select. Most tapes require two to three times fullness.

MATERIALS

- Decorator fabric.
- Lining fabric, if desired.
- Curtain rod or pole set with rings.
- Self-styling tape; use sew-in tape for unlined or lined curtains, or use fusible tape for unlined curtains.
- Drapery weights.

CUTTING DIRECTIONS

Allow for two to three times fullness, depending on the desired look and the type of self-styling tape. If a hand-draw pole set is used, determine the cut width of the decorator fabric by multiplying the width of the pole between brackets times the desired fullness and add 6" (15 cm) for each panel to allow for 1½" (3.8 cm) double-fold side hems. If it is necessary to piece fabric widths together to make each panel, also add 1" (2.5 cm) for each seam. If a standard or decorative curtain rod is used, also add twice the projection of the rod to this measurement to allow for returns.

If using a standard curtain rod, determine the finished length of the curtain by measuring from the top of the rod to where you want the lower edge of the drapery; then add ½" (1.3 cm) so the drapery will extend above the rod. Or if using a decorative curtain rod or a pole set with rings, measure from the pin holes in the glides or rings to the desired length. The cut length of the decorator fabric is equal to the desired finished length of the curtain plus ¾" (2 cm) for turn-under at the upper edge and 8" (20.5 cm) for a 4" (10 cm) double-fold hem at the lower edge.

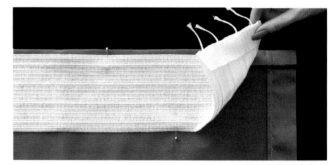

1 Seam fabric widths, if necessary, for each curtain panel. At the lower edge, press under 4" (10 cm) twice to wrong side; stitch to make double-fold hem, using blindstitch or straight stitch. Press under 1½" (3.8 cm) twice on sides; tack drapery weights inside the side hems, about 3" (7.5 cm) from the lower edge. Stitch side hems. Press under ¾" (2 cm) on upper edge of curtain panel.

2 Cut shirring tape to width of hemmed panel plus 2" (5 cm). Turn under 1" (2.5 cm) on each end of tape, and use pin to pick out cords. Position tape right side up on wrong side of panel, with upper edge of tape ¼" (6 mm) from folded edge of panel.

4 Knot all cords together, or knot them in pairs, at each end of shirring tape. At one end, pull evenly on cords to shirr fabric, adjusting width of heading to desired finished width.

3 Stitch sew-in tape (**a**) in place next to cords. Or fuse fusible tape (**b**) in place; then insert a strip of fusible web at ends along edges, and fuse.

5 Knot cords in pairs at side of curtain. Cut off excess cord length, or conceal cords behind panel. If cords are not cut, panel can be smoothed for laundering.

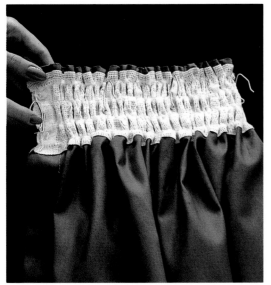

6 Insert drapery pins at ends of panels and at 3" (7.5 cm) intervals. Or if self-styling tape has loops, insert drapery pins into them.

7 Insert drapery pins into eyes of the glides on a decorative curtain rod **(a)** or eyes of rings for a pole set **(b).** Or hook pins over a standard curtain rod **(c).**

HOW TO MAKE LINED CURTAINS USING SELF-STYLING TAPE

CUTTING DIRECTIONS

Determine the width and length of the decorator fabric as for unlined curtains, opposite. The cut width of the lining is equal to the cut width of the decorator fabric. The cut length of the lining is 5¾" (14.5 cm) shorter than the cut length of the decorator fabric; this allows for a 2" (5 cm) double-fold hem and for the lining to be 1" (2.5 cm) shorter than the finished curtain.

1 Seam decorator fabric widths, if necessary, for each curtain panel; repeat for lining panel. At lower edge of curtain panel, press under 4" (10 cm) twice to wrong side; stitch to make double-fold hem. Repeat for lining panel, pressing under 2" (5 cm) twice.

2 Press under ¾" (2 cm) on upper edge of curtain panel only. Place curtain panel and lining panel wrong sides together, matching raw edges at sides and with raw edge of lining at pressed foldline; fold edge of curtain panel over lining, and pin in place. At the bottom, the lining panel will be 1" (2.5 cm) shorter than the curtain panel.

3 Press under 1½" (3.8 cm) twice on sides; tack drapery weights inside the side hems, about 3" (7.5 cm) from lower edge. Stitch to make double-fold hems. Finish the curtains as in steps 2 to 7, opposite.

PLEATED DRAPERIES

Pleated draperies are a classic, ever-popular window treatment. Installed on traverse rods, they let in light when opened and offer privacy when closed. The pleats provide fullness to the draperies in uniform, graceful folds. The styling of pleated draperies can be varied by changing the pleat style and the pleat spacing (pages 44 and 45).

The instructions that follow are for a pair of drapery panels mounted on a two-way-draw traverse rod. When mounting the drapery rod, allow for the stacking space (page 19) at the sides of the window so the draperies will clear the window when they are open. The actual stacking space varies depending on the weight of the fabric, the fullness of the draperies, and whether or not they are lined, but it is estimated at one-third the width of the window; allow for one-half of the stacking space on each side of the window.

If the draperies will hang from a conventional traverse rod, determine the finished length by measuring from the top of the rod to where you want the lower edge of the draperies; then add ½" (1.3 cm) so the draperies will extend above the rod. If the draperies will hang from a decorative rod, measure from the bottom of the rod to the desired finished length. If the draperies will hang from a pole set with rings, measure from the pin holes in the rings to the desired finished length.

Two and one-half times fullness is used for most draperies, but for sheers, three times fullness may be used. For lace draperies, use two and one-half times fullness so the pattern of the lace is noticeable in the finished draperies.

After the drapery panels are seamed and hemmed, use the Pleats Worksheet to determine the number and size of the pleats and the spaces between them.

MATERIALS

- Decorator fabric.
- Lining fabric, if desired.
- Buckram, 4" (10 cm) wide.
- Conventional or decorative traverse rod.
- Drapery weights; drapery hooks.

CUTTING DIRECTIONS

Use the Fabric Worksheet on page 38 to determine and record the necessary measurements. Several widths of fabric are often required. Cut the number of fabric widths you need to the calculated cut length of the draperies. If the number of widths is an odd number, divide one of the widths in half, and add one half to each of the two drapery panels.

FABRIC WORKSHEET

Drapery Length	in. (cm)
Desired finished length (as determined on page 37)	
8" (20.5 cm) for heading	+
8" (20.5 cm) for 4" (10 cm) double-fold lower hem	+
Cut drapery length	=
Drapery Width	
Rod width (from end bracket to end bracket on conventional rods; from end ring to end ring on decorative rods)	
Allowance for two returns [projection of rod plus ½" (1.3 cm) for each return]	+
3½" (9 cm) for overlap	+
Finished drapery width	=
Total Number of Drapery Fabric Widths	
Finished drapery width multiplied by 2½ to 3 times for fullness	
Divided by width of fabric	÷
Total number of fabric widths needed, rounded up or down to nearest full width	=
Number of Drapery Fabric Widths per Panel	
Total number of fabric widths	
Divided by 2	÷
Number of fabric widths per panel	=

LINING FABRIC WORKSHEET

Lining Length	in. (cm)
Finished drapery length	
4" (10 cm) for 2" (5 cm) double-fold lower hem	+
Cut lining length	=
Number of Lining Widths	
Calculate as for Total Number of Drapery Fabric Widths (above).	

PLEATS WORKSHEET

After completing step 4 (opposite), use this worksheet to determine the number and size of pleats and the spaces between them. The recommended amount of fabric required for each pleat is 4" to 6" (10 to 15 cm). The recommended space between pleats is 3½" to 4" (9 to 10 cm). If the calculation from the worksheet results in pleats or spaces that are greater than the amount recommended, add one pleat and space. If the calculation results in pleats or spaces smaller than the amount recommended, subtract one pleat and space.

Finished Panel Width	in. (cm)
Finished drapery width (figured left)	
Divided by 2	÷
Finished panel width	=
Number of Pleats per Panel	
Number of drapery fabric widths per panel (figured left)	
Multiplied by number of pleats per width*	×
Number of pleats per panel	=
Space Between Pleats	
Finished panel width (figured above)	
Overlap and returns (figured left)	-
Width to be pleated	=
Divided by number of spaces per panel (one less than number of pleats per panel)	÷
Space between pleats	=
Pleat Size	
Flat width of hemmed panel (from step 4)	
Finished panel width (figured above)	-
Total amount allowed for pleats	=
Divided by number of pleats per panel (figured above)	÷
Pleat size	=

Figure 5 pleats per width of 48" (122 cm) fabric, 6 pleats per width of 54" (137 cm) fabric. For example, for 54" (137 cm) fabric, 3 widths per panel = 18 pleats. If you have a half width of fabric, figure 2 or 3 pleats in that half width.

HOW TO SEW UNLINED PLEATED DRAPERIES

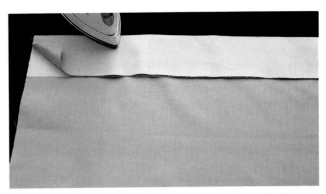

1 Seam widths together as necessary, removing selvages to prevent puckering; finish seam allowances by serging or zigzagging. Press seams open or to outer edge of drapery. At lower edge, press under 4" (10 cm) twice to wrong side; stitch to make double-fold hem, using blindstitch or straight stitch.

2 Cut buckram the width of each drapery panel. Place buckram even with upper edge of drapery panel, on wrong side. Fold heading and buckram to wrong side; press. Fold again, encasing buckram in fabric; press. Pin or hand-baste in place.

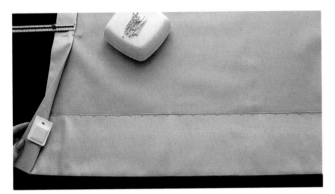

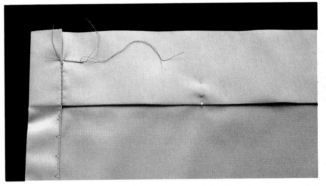

3 Press under 1½" (3.8 cm) twice on sides. Tack drapery weights inside the side hems, about 3" (7.5 cm) from lower edge.

4 Stitch double-fold side hems, using blindstitch or straight stitch; hand-stitch hem in place at heading. Determine the number and size of pleats and spaces between them as in Pleats Worksheet, opposite.

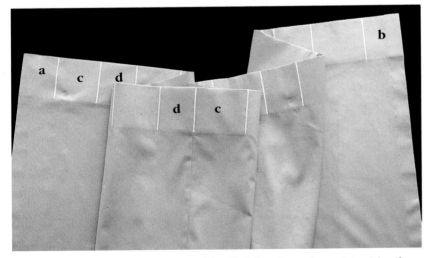

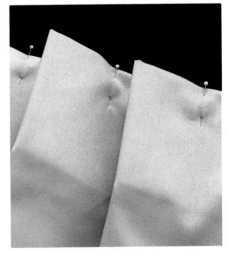

5 Mark the return **(a)** and overlap **(b)** of left-hand panel, on right side of fabric, using chalk. Mark pleats **(c)** and spaces **(d)**, with one pleat next to return and one next to overlap; seams should fall on right-hand marking of a space. Pleat size can vary slightly and be adjusted as necessary within each fabric width; keep the spaces uniform. With panels right sides together, transfer markings to right-hand panel.

6 Fold each pleat by bringing pleat lines together; pin. Crease buckram on the fold.

(Continued)

7 Stitch on pleat line from top of heading to lower edge of buckram; backstitch to secure.

8 Check finished width of panel along heading. Adjust size of a few pleats if necessary to adjust width of panel.

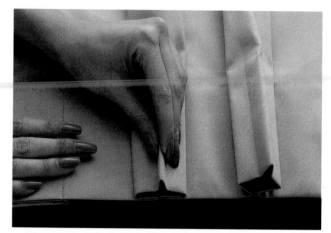

9 Divide each stitched pleat into three even pleats. Open the pleat at the top of the heading. Pinch the folds of the pleats.

10 Press center fold straight down to meet the pleat stitching line. Crease pleats that form at the sides.

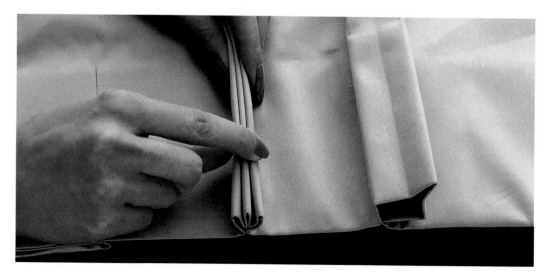

11 Pinch outer folds up to meet center fold. Finger-press three pleats together, making sure they are all even.

12 Bar tack pleats by machine just above lower edge of buckram; or tack pleats by hand, using stabstitch and heavy-duty thimble.

13 Insert drapery hooks, with one hook at each pleat and one hook near each end of the panel. On a conventional traverse rod **(a),** top of hook is 1¾" (4.5 cm) from upper edge of overdrapery or 1¼" (3.2 cm) from upper edge of underdrapery. On a decorator traverse rod **(b),** top of hook is ¾" to 1" (2 to 2.5 cm) from upper edge. On a pole set with rings **(c),** top of hook is ¼" (6 mm) from upper edge. (Shown on traverse rods for clarity.)

14 Crease the buckram midway between each pleat; fold it forward if a conventional traverse rod is being used, or fold it to the back if a decorative traverse rod is being used. This is often referred to as "cracking" the buckram. After cracking the buckram, press draperies, using warm, dry iron.

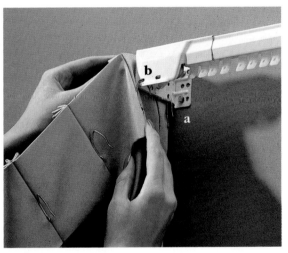

15 Hang the end hook at return in hole on the side of the bracket **(a).** Hang the hook of first pleat in hole at front corner of the bracket **(b).**

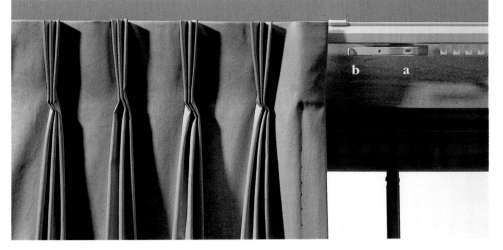

16 Hang the hooks for middle pleats on glides; remove any glides that are not used. Hang the hook for last pleat in first hole of master slide **(a).** Hang the end hook on overlap of drapery in end hole of master slide **(b).** Pinch the hooks on the master slides to keep them from catching when the draperies are drawn; also, pull the front master slide forward, if necessary.

(Continued)

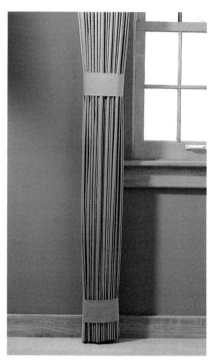

17 Open draperies completely into stacked position; check heading to be sure buckram is folded as it was cracked in step 14. Starting at heading, guide pleats into evenly spaced soft folds of equal depth; follow grainline of fabric to keep pleats perpendicular to floor.

18 Staple narrow strip of matching fabric or muslin around drapery panel, midway between heading and hem, to hold pleats in place. Do not secure fabric too tightly, to prevent creasing the folds.

19 Staple second strip of fabric at hemline. Check to see that draperies hang straight down from rod. Leave draperies in this position for two weeks to set the pleats. In humid conditions, one week may be sufficient.

HOW TO SEW LINED PLEATED DRAPERIES

1 Stitch drapery fabric as on page 39, step 1. Seam lining widths together as necessary, removing selvages to prevent puckering; finish seam allowances by serging or zigzagging, if desired. At lower edge, press under 2" (5 cm) twice to wrong side; stitch to make double-fold hem, using blindstitch or straight stitch.

2 Place drapery panel on large flat surface. Lay lining panel on top of drapery panel, wrong sides together, with lower edge of lining 1" (2.5 cm) above lower edge of drapery panel; raw edges will be even at sides.

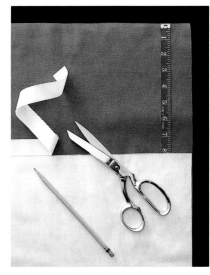

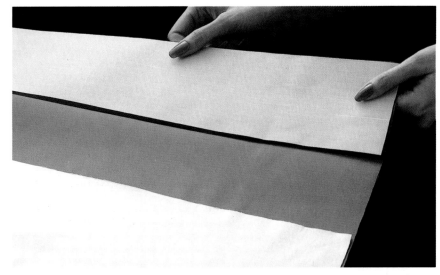

3 Mark lining panel 8" (20.5 cm) from upper edge of drapery panel. Trim on marked line.

4 Cut buckram the width of each drapery panel. Place buckram even with upper edge of drapery panel, on wrong side. Fold heading and buckram to wrong side; press.

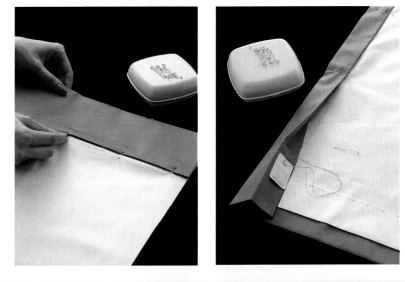

5 Fold again, encasing the buckram in fabric; press. Lining edge will be even with the top of the heading. Pin or hand-baste in place.

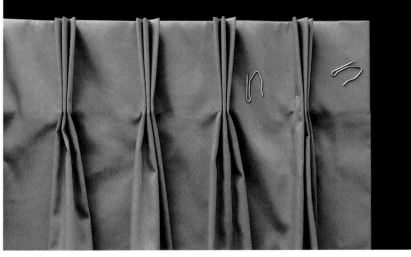

6 Press under 1½" (3.8 cm) twice on sides, folding lining and drapery panels as one fabric. Tack the drapery weights inside the side hems, about 3" (7.5 cm) from lower edge.

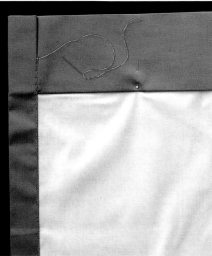

7 Stitch double-fold side hems, using blindstitch or straight stitch; hand-stitch side hem in place at heading.

8 Finish draperies as on pages 39 to 42, steps 5 to 19.

Grouped pleats *(above) add interest to drapery headings. Achieve this look by sewing pleated draperies (page 37), varying the spacing between the pleats as in step 5 on page 39.*

Double pinch pleats *(left) have two pleats, instead of three, for a casual look (page 46).*

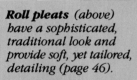

Roll pleats *(above) have a sophisticated, traditional look and provide soft, yet tailored, detailing (page 46).*

Goblet pleats *(right) give a soft look to the draperies (page 47). Because goblet pleats do not stack as tightly as pinch pleats, you may want to allow extra stackback (page 19) so the draperies will clear the window when open.*

HOW TO SEW DRAPERIES WITH ROLL PLEATS

1 Follow steps 1 to 8 on pages 39 to 40 for unlined draperies. Or for lined draperies, follow steps 1 to 7 on pages 42 and 43 and steps 5 to 8 on pages 39 and 40. Open the pleat at top of heading; holding two fingers under pleat, flatten pleat so it is centered over seamline.

2 Roll sides of pleat so folded edges are even with stitching.

3 Tack pleats as on page 41, step 12; position stitches near folded edge. Insert hooks and install draperies as on pages 41 and 42, steps 13 to 19.

HOW TO SEW DRAPERIES WITH DOUBLE PINCH PLEATS

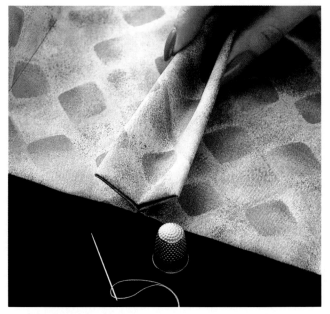

1 Follow steps 1 to 8 on pages 39 to 40 for unlined draperies. Or for lined draperies, follow steps 1 to 7 on pages 42 and 43 and steps 5 to 8 on pages 39 and 40. Open the pleat at top of heading. Flatten pleat so it is centered over seamline.

2 Bring folded edges up. Finger-press the two pleats together, making sure they are even. Tack pleats as on page 41, step 12. Insert hooks and install draperies as on pages 41 and 42, steps 13 to 19.

HOW TO SEW DRAPERIES WITH GOBLET PLEATS

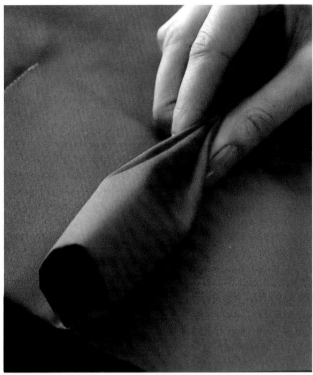

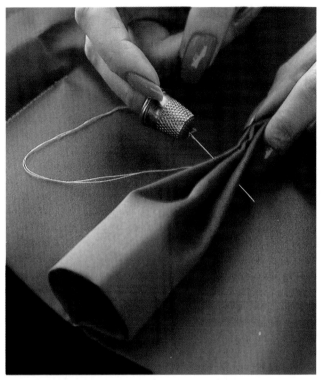

1 Follow steps 1 to 8 on pages 39 to 40 for unlined draperies. Or for lined draperies, follow steps 1 to 7 on pages 42 and 43 and steps 5 to 8 on pages 39 and 40. Open the pleat at top of heading. Pinch fabric at bottom of buckram into three or four small pleats.

2 Tack pleats by hand, using stabstitch and heavy-duty thimble; or bar tack pleats by machine just above lower edge of buckram.

3 Form pleat into rounded, goblet shape. Hand-stitch pleat along upper edge of drapery, as shown, up to ½" (1.3 cm) on each side of stitching line. Press draperies, using warm, dry iron.

4 Insert tissue paper into pleats, to ensure they retain goblet shape. Insert hooks and install draperies as on pages 41 and 42, steps 13 to 19. Remove tissue paper when draperies are cleaned.

Designer Window Treatments

TIE-TAB CURTAINS

For an informal look, make tie-tab curtains. Used with a pole set or decorative curtain rod, this simple, no-fuss curtain has plenty of style. Lined tie-tab curtains drape well and are easy to sew. The size of the tabs and the spacing between them may vary, depending on the look you want.

MATERIALS

• Decorator fabric and lining fabric, for curtain panels.

• Matching or contrasting lining, for tabs.

• Pole set or decorative curtain rod.

• Drapery weights.

CUTTING DIRECTIONS

Determine the finished length of the curtain by measuring from the bottom of the pole or rod to where you want the lower edge of the curtain; then subtract the distance or space you want between the bottom of the pole and the upper edge of the curtain. Determine the width of the hem at the lower edge. A 4" (10 cm) double-fold hem is often used for the decorator fabric and a 2" (5 cm) double-fold hem for the lining.

The cut length of the decorator fabric is equal to the desired finished length of the curtain plus twice the width of the hem plus ½" (1.3 cm) for the seam allowance at the upper edge.

The cut width of the decorator fabric is equal to two or two and one-half times the width of the pole or rod. After multiplying the width of the pole times the desired fullness, add 6" (15 cm) for each panel to allow for 1½" (3.8 cm) double-fold side hems. If it is necessary to piece fabric widths together to make each panel, also add 1" (2.5 cm) for each seam.

The cut length of the lining is 5" (12.5 cm) shorter than the cut length of the decorator fabric; this allows for a 2" (5 cm) double-fold hem at the lower edge and for the lining to be 1" (2.5 cm) shorter than the curtain when it is finished. The cut width of the lining is equal to the cut width of the decorator fabric.

Decide on the finished width you want the tabs to be. Then determine the spacing and number of tabs for each curtain panel; two tabs are placed at each location. Evenly space the tabs 3" to 8" (7.5 to 20.5 cm) apart, depending on the look you want.

Cut one strip of decorator fabric and one of matching or contrasting lining for each tab, with each fabric strip ½" (1.3 cm) wider and ¾" (2 cm) longer than the desired finished size.

Determine tab length by pinning fabric strips over pole or rod, with tabs tied in knot or bow as desired; mark tab at desired distance from pole, using pins. Untie, and cut strips to marked length plus ¾" (2 cm) to allow for seam allowances.

HOW TO SEW TIE-TAB CURTAINS

1 Place one strip of decorator fabric and one of lining right sides together, matching raw edges. Stitch ¼" (6 mm) seam around long sides and one end of tab. Repeat for remaining tabs. Trim corners, turn tabs right side out, and press.

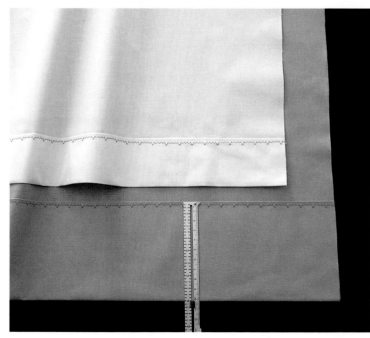

2 Seam decorator fabric widths, if necessary, for each curtain panel; repeat for lining panel. At lower edge of curtain panel, press under 4" (10 cm) twice to wrong side; stitch to make double-fold hem, using blindstitch or straight stitch. Repeat for hem on lining panel, pressing under 2" (5 cm) twice.

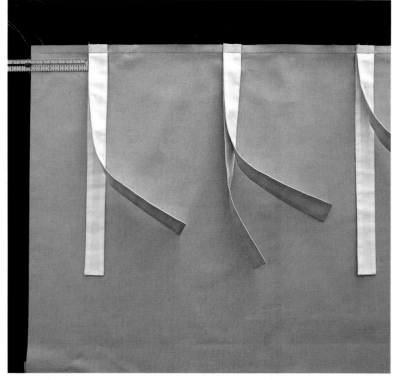

3 Pin tabs to right side of curtain panel at upper edge, with raw edges matching and right sides of tabs facing down; place two tabs at each placement. Tabs at ends must be placed 3" (7.5 cm) from each side; space remaining tabs evenly between the end tabs. Machine-baste the tabs in place.

4 Place curtain panel and lining panel right sides together, matching raw edges at sides and upper edge; pin. At the bottom, the lining panel will be 1" (2.5 cm) shorter than the curtain panel.

5 Stitch ½" (1.3 cm) seam at upper edge. Press seam allowances open; then fold lining to wrong side of curtain, and press.

6 Press under 1½" (3.8 cm) twice on sides, folding lining and curtain panel as one fabric. Tack drapery weights inside the side hems, about 3" (7.5 cm) from lower edge.

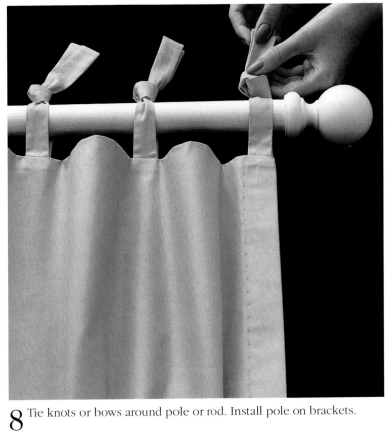

7 Stitch to make double-fold side hems, using blindstitch or straight stitch.

8 Tie knots or bows around pole or rod. Install pole on brackets.

TIE-TAB
CURTAIN
VARIATIONS

Tailored tabs (above) give a look of simplicity to this curtain. Instead of tying the tabs, both ends are inserted into the seam at the upper edge of the curtain. One tab is inserted at each placement mark; the finished size of the tabs shown here is 2½" × 9" (6.5 × 23 cm). The space between the tabs is 4½" (11.5 cm).

Alternating tabs (right) are tied together to create the uniform, soft folds. The curtain has two and one-half times fullness. Only one tab is inserted at each placement mark on this curtain; the finished size of the tabs shown here is 1½" × 11" (3.8 × 28 cm). An even number of tabs is used for this curtain, and the space between the tabs is 3" (7.5 cm).

Knotted tabs (opposite) in two colors are tied close to the curtains for a new look. The finished size of the tabs that wrap around the pole is 1½" × 15" (3.8 × 38 cm); the front tabs are 3" (7.5 cm) shorter. The space between the tabs is 6" (15 cm).

RELAXED
ROMAN SHADES

The relaxed Roman shade is simple yet updated in styling and complements many decors. A pleated border drapes gently at the lower edge to soften the otherwise tailored look. This style has only two rows of rings, making it quick to construct.

A straight valance can be added to an outside-mounted shade. The valance has returns at the sides, to conceal the mounting board and hardware.

For a pleasing drape at the lower edge, the finished width of the shade should not exceed 48" (122 cm); this size can be cut from one width of 54" (137 cm) decorator fabric.

Before making this project, read pages 16 and 17 about covering and installing mounting boards. For inside-mounted shades, steps 1 and 2 on page 17 can be completed before the shade is made; or for outside-mounted shades, steps 1 to 4 on page 17 can be completed.

MATERIALS

FOR ROMAN SHADE

• Decorator fabric.

• Lining fabric.

• Mounting board, cut as on pages 16 and 17.

• Angle irons, shorter than projection of mounting board; flat-head wood screws; two screw eyes.

• Two lengths of shade cord, each cord long enough to run up the shade, across the top, and partway down the side.

• 1/2" (1.3 cm) plastic rings; two rings for every 6" (15 cm) of shade length.

• One 3/8" (1 cm) brass weight rod, cut 1/2" (1.3 cm) shorter than finished width of shade.

• Tacks, or staple gun and staples.

• Awning cleat.

FOR VALANCE

• Strip of 1/2" × 3/4" (1.3 × 2 cm) board, such as pine parting stop, cut to same length as mounting board.

• Three 8 × 1" (2.5 cm) wallboard screws.

• Drill for predrilling screw holes; 5/32" (3.8 mm) drill bit.

CUTTING DIRECTIONS

Determine the finished width and finished length of the shade; the pleats at the lower edge will drape 2" (5 cm) below the finished length at the middle of the shade.

Cut the decorator fabric for the shade 6" (15 cm) wider than the finished width. Cut the length of the decorator fabric to the finished length of the shade plus the projection of the mounting board plus 1½" (3.8 cm) for the rod pocket and 21" (53.5 cm) for the draped pleats at the lower edge. The cut width of the lining is equal to the finished width of the shade; cut the lining the same length as the decorator fabric.

HOW TO SEW A RELAXED ROMAN SHADE

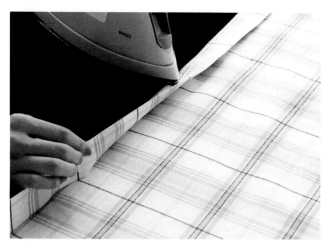

1 Press under scant 1½" (3.8 cm) on sides of decorator fabric; then press under 1½" (3.8 cm).

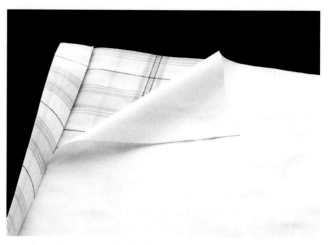

2 Place lining on shade fabric, wrong sides together, matching upper and lower edges; at sides, place lining under hems up to second foldline.

3 Pin side hems to lining; blindstitch or fuse in place.

4 Press under ½" (1.3 cm) of lining and decorator fabric at lower edge. Then press under 1" (2.5 cm), forming rod pocket. Stitch close to first fold.

5 Mark locations for first row of rings with X's spaced 6" (15 cm) apart vertically. Starting at bottom of shade, mark two X's 1½" (3.8 cm) from side of shade. Mark next two X's 1¾" (4.5 cm) from side. Mark remaining X's 2½" (6.5 cm) from side. Repeat for row of rings on opposite side of shade.

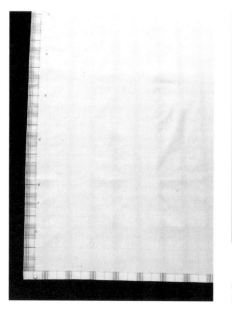

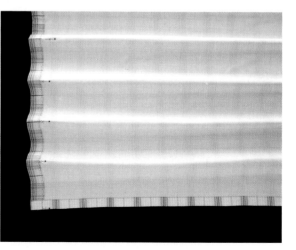

6 Pin through both layers of fabric at center of ring markings, with pins parallel to bottom of shade. Fold shade in accordion pleats at pins, to position shade for attaching rings.

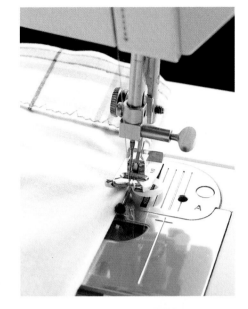

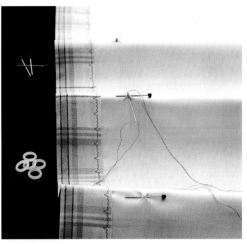

7 Attaching rings by machine. Attach rings by placing fold under the presser foot with ring next to fold. Set zigzag stitch at widest setting; set stitch length at 0. Stitch over the ring, securing it with about eight stitches. Secure the stitches by stitching in place for two or three stitches, with stitch width and length set at 0.

7 Attaching rings by hand. Tack rings by hand, using double strand of thread, stitching in place through both fabric layers for four or five stitches.

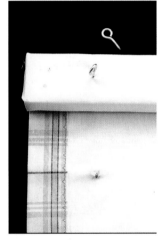

8 Finish raw edges at upper edge of shade by serging or zigzagging. Cover mounting board (page 16), if desired; staple or tack shade to top of mounting board, aligning upper edge of shade to back edge of board.

9 Install screw eyes on mounting board, aligning them with rows of rings.

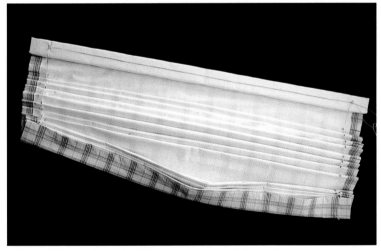

10 Tie lower five rings of each row together with a length of shade cord, using an overhand knot. Apply fabric glue to knot and end of cord to prevent knot from slipping.

11 Run cord through remaining rings and through screw eyes; run cord from first screw eye across the top and through second screw eye. With shade pulled flat, cut cords, leaving excess length at the side for raising and lowering the shade.

(Continued)

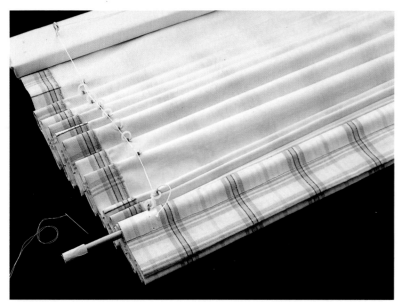

12 File ends of weight rod smooth, or cover ends with tape. Insert rod in rod pocket; hand-stitch ends of rod pocket closed. Make valance (below), if desired.

13 Mount shade as for inside-mounted board on page 17, step 3, or as for outside-mounted board on page 17, step 5. Adjust cords with shade lowered so the tension on each cord is equal. Insert ends of cord into top of drapery pull; knot ends.

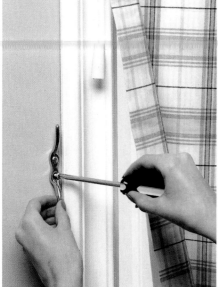

14 Screw awning cleat into window frame or wall.

15 Pull shade into raised position; wrap cords around awning cleat. Arrange folds. Leave shade in this position for two weeks to set the folds. In humid conditions, one week may be sufficient.

HOW TO SEW A VALANCE

CUTTING DIRECTIONS

Cut the decorator fabric for the valance, with the width of the fabric equal to the finished width of the shade plus twice the projection of the mounting board plus 2½" (6.5 cm); this allows for seam allowances, ease, and returns, including the ½" (1.3 cm) projection of the parting stop. To determine the cut length of the valance, add the projection of the mounting board plus ½" (1.3 cm) for the projection of the parting stop to the desired finished length of the valance; multiply this measurement by two.

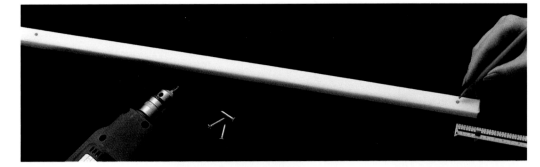

1 Cover parting stop with fabric as for mounting board (page 16), if desired. Mark screw locations on ¾" (2 cm) side of parting stop, with one mark at center and one mark 1" (2.5 cm) from each end.

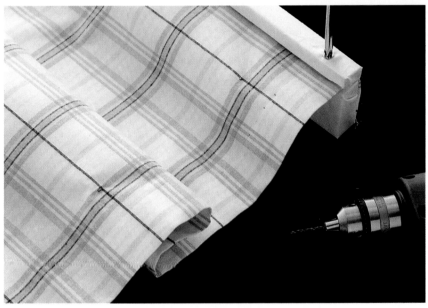

2 Place parting stop on front of shade, aligning upper edges. At markings, predrill through parting stop and into mounting board, using 5⁄32" (3.8 mm) drill bit. Attach parting stop to mounting board with screws.

3 Fold the valance fabric in half lengthwise, right sides together; stitch ½" (1.3 cm) seams at short ends.

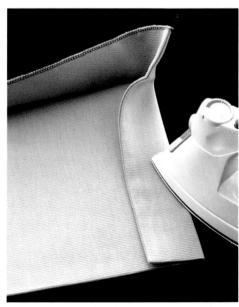

4 Turn valance right side out; press. Finish raw edges by serging or zigzagging them together. Press under finished upper edge an amount equal to projection; press returns at sides.

5 Staple valance to top of mounting board, placing pressed fold along front edge of board; upper edge of shade will be aligned with back edge of board. Miter corners; staple in place on top of board. Secure returns to sides of mounting board, using hot glue, if necessary, to keep returns flat.

LACE CLOUD SHADES

This delicate lace cloud shade hangs as a softly shirred panel when lowered full length. When raised, the bottom of the shade forms soft, cloudlike poufs. The shade can be used alone or as an undertreatment.

The top of the lace panel is gathered with shirring tape and attached to a mounting board with adhesive-backed hook and loop tape. The shade is raised by pulling on invisible monofilament fishing lines.

Select a lace with a decorative border. To use the border at the lower edge and prevent seams in the shade, select lace yardage that is wide enough so the length of the shade can be cut crosswise on the fabric. Or choose a panel of lace that is large enough for the shade.

The size of each scallop in the completed shade is usually from 9" to 12" (23 to 30.5 cm). Based on the size of the scallops, decide on the number of scallops in the shade.

Before making this project, read pages 16 and 17 about covering and installing mounting boards. For inside-mounted shades, steps 1 and 2 on page 17 can be completed before the shade is made; or for outside-mounted shades, steps 1 to 4 on page 17 can be completed.

MATERIALS

- Lace yardage or lace panel with decorative border.
- Fabric to match lace, for covering mounting board.
- Sheer, three-cord shirring tape.
- Monofilament fishing line, 30-lb. (13.5-k) test; ¾-size bell swivel sinkers, painted to match lace.
- Adhesive-backed hook and loop tape.

- Mounting board, cut as on pages 16 and 17.
- Angle irons, shorter than width of mounting board; flat-head wood screws.
- Screw eyes; large wooden bead; awning cleat; weighted drapery pull.
- Heavy-duty stapler and staples.

HOW TO MAKE A LACE CLOUD SHADE (INSIDE MOUNT)

CUTTING DIRECTIONS

Allow for two to two and one-half times fullness, depending on the desired look and the type of shirring tape used. To determine the cut width of the shade, multiply the width of the mounting board times the desired fullness; then add 4" (10 cm) to allow for 1" (2.5 cm) double-fold side hems. The cut length is ¾" (2 cm) longer than the desired finished length.

1 Press under 1" (2.5 cm) twice on sides of panel; stitch hems. Press under ¾" (2 cm) on upper edge. Cut shirring tape to width of hemmed panel plus 2" (5 cm). Turn under 1" (2.5 cm) on ends of tape; use pin to pick out cords. Position tape right side up on wrong side of panel, with upper edge of tape ¼" (6 mm) from fold. Stitch along upper and lower edges of tape.

2 Pin-mark placement for outer rows of fishing line just inside each side hem, placing safety pins (indicated by green dots) on wrong side at 5" to 6" (12.5 to 15 cm) intervals, with first pin 2" (5 cm) from lower edge of shade. Measure distance between outer rows; divide this measurement by desired number of scallops. Pin-mark remaining rows this distance apart, positioning pins as for outer rows. Do not place pins within 5" (12.5 cm) of shirring tape.

(Continued)

3 Weave fishing line for first row in and out of lace at pin marks, leaving 12" (30.5 cm) tail at lower end; extend length of cord at top of shade so it is long enough to run across mounting board and partway down the opposite side.

4 Insert fishing line at lower edge of shade into eye of sinker. Twist end around fishing line four or five times. Secure line by bringing end through loop; pull tight. Cut off excess line. (Tinted fishing line is used to show detail.)

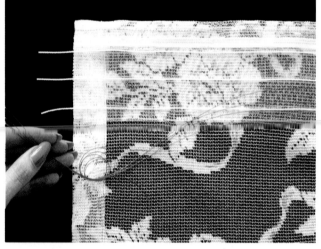

5 Repeat steps 3 and 4 for remaining rows; knot fishing lines together at side of shade.

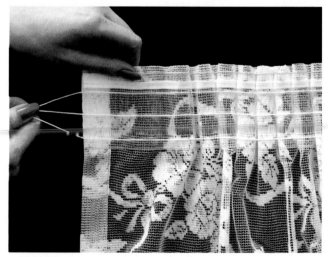

6 Knot cords together at each end of shirring tape. At one end, pull evenly on cords to shirr fabric, adjusting width of heading to measurement of inside window frame. Knot cords together close to shade; cut off excess cord.

7 Cut hook and loop tape to finished width of shade. Adhere hook side of tape to front edge of mounting board; reinforce with staples. Adhere loop side to shirring tape at upper edge of shade. Attach shade to covered mounting board, aligning strips of hook and loop tape.

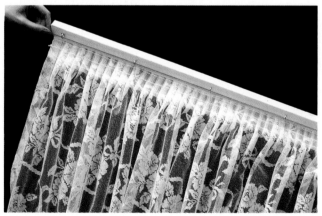

8 Insert screw eyes into mounting board, centering them on bottom of board and placing one screw eye above each row of fishing line. Untie knot at ends of fishing line; run fishing lines through screw eyes.

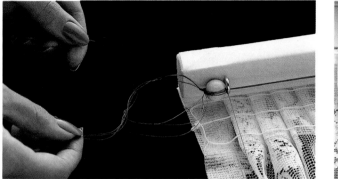

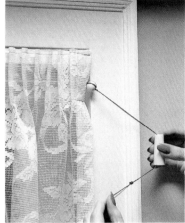

9 Adjust fishing lines so the tension on each fishing line will be equal when shade is installed. Knot fishing lines just below screw eye. Secure a bead next to knot.

10 Install the mounting board with shade as for inside-mounted board on page 17, step 3. Trim ends even at side of shade, leaving excess length for pulling. Braid fishing lines. Insert braided line into weighted drapery pull; knot end. Screw awning cleat into window frame.

HOW TO MAKE A LACE CLOUD SHADE (OUTSIDE MOUNT)

CUTTING DIRECTIONS

Allow for two to two and one-half times fullness, depending on the desired look and the type of shirring tape used. To determine the cut width of the shade, add twice the projection of the mounting board to the width of the board; then multiply this measurement times the desired fullness and add 4" (10 cm) to allow for 1" (2.5 cm) double-fold side hems.

The cut length of the shade is ¾" (2 cm) longer than the desired finished length.

1 Follow steps 1 to 5 on pages 63 and 64 for inside-mounted shade. Knot cords together at each end of shirring tape. At one end, pull evenly on cords to shirr fabric, adjusting width of heading to the finished width of shade including returns. Knot cords together close to shade; cut off excess cord.

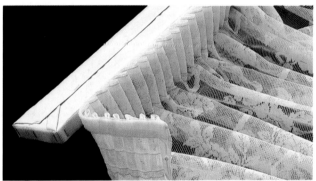

2 Cut hook and loop tape to the finished width of shade including returns. Adhere hook side of tape to front and side edges of mounting board; reinforce with staples. Adhere loop side to shirring tape at upper edge of shade. Attach shade to covered mounting board, aligning strips of hook and loop tape.

3 Insert screw eyes into mounting board, centering them on bottom of board and placing one screw eye above each of the middle rows of fishing line. Also insert one screw eye, centered on bottom of board, near each end; these eyes are for the end rows of fishing line.

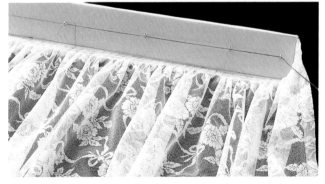

4 Untie knot at ends of fishing line; run fishing lines through screw eyes, as shown. Complete shade as in steps 9 and 10, above.

CURTAINS FROM SHEETS

Create curtains quickly, using decorative sheets with embellished edges. For a romantic window treatment, choose ruffled sheets or sheets with lace trims. For a more tailored look, select sheets with flat or pleated borders. And for imaginative valances, use pillow shams that coordinate.

The decorative edge of the sheet may be used at the inner, upper, or lower edge of a curtain panel, depending on the style of the window treatment. Decide where you want to position the decorative edge and how much fullness you want the curtain to have. Then determine the sheet size you will need, allowing for any headings, rod pockets, and hems.

For best results, purchase good-quality sheets with a high thread count. When selecting patterned sheets, keep in mind that some one-way designs may not be suitable if the sheet will be turned sideways or upside down. If the ruffle or border will be used vertically on the curtain, the width of the sheet must be long enough for the cut length of the curtain.

Cutwork borders become the decorative lower edges of rod-pocket curtains and valance.

Sheets with printed borders create curtains with a tailored look. So the border can be used as the heading of the curtain, a separate piece of fabric is stitched on the wrong side of the sheet for the rod pocket.

Pillow sham (opposite) makes a coordinated top treatment for curtains from sheets. Fold the sham diagonally and secure it to a decorative wood pole, using double-stick tape.

Cloud valance *(page 71), with soft poufs or scallops, is shirred onto a curtain rod. The stretched rod-pocket curtain is sewn as on page 31.*

For kitchen windows, towels become creative window treatments, giving a casual, carefree look. Towels work well for small rod-pocket curtain panels and valances. They are available in coordinating patterns, some with contrasting borders to make curtains that have the look of banding.

Linen or linen-blend towels will maintain a crisp look. Before making the curtains, launder the towels to preshrink them. Then press them, using spray starch.

Determine the number of towels needed, depending on the style of window treatment and the size of the towels. Keep in mind that the towels can be turned sideways.

Whenever possible, take advantage of the existing hems in the towels for a homespun look. If several towels are seamed together for curtain panels and valances, rehem the lower edges for a more finished appearance.

CURTAINS FROM KITCHEN TOWELS

Tieback curtains (page 70) have a tailored look. The towels have been lengthened by seaming two towels together; the seams are concealed under the tiebacks.

Rod-pocket cafes and valance (upper right) are sewn as for basic rod-pocket curtains (page 25); if you are using the existing hems in the towels, do not add hem allowances.

Cafe curtains are quick and easy to sew. For cafes with rings, stitch a 2" to 3" (5 to 7.5 cm) hem at the upper edge of the curtain panels and sew rings to each towel. For tie-tab cafes, stitch horizontal buttonholes at the top of the kitchen-towel panels, thread ribbons through the buttonholes, and tie ribbons to a decorative rod.

HOW TO MAKE TIEBACK CURTAINS FROM KITCHEN TOWELS

MATERIALS

- Four kitchen towels for two curtain panels.
- One matching or coordinating towel for tiebacks.

- Curtain rod.
- Tieback rings; tenter hooks or cup hooks.

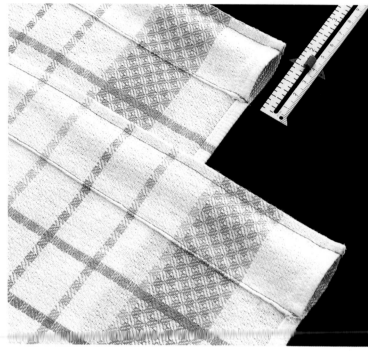

1 Fold under upper edge of two towels an amount equal to desired depth of heading and rod pocket; press. Stitch heading and rod pocket as on page 26, steps 3 and 4.

2 Insert the curtain rod through the rod pocket. Determine center of tieback placement; mark on outer edge. Measure from mark straight down to desired finished length of curtain.

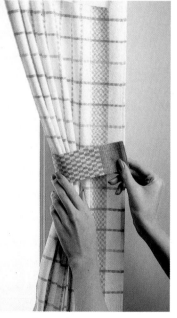

3 Cut towels ½" (1.3 cm) below marked tieback placement. Cut two remaining towels for curtain panels to measurement determined in step 2 plus ½" (1.3 cm). Stitch upper and lower sections, right sides together, in ½" (1.3 cm) seam. Finish seam allowances, and press seam open.

4 Make tailored tiebacks (page 104). Hang curtains, and secure tiebacks as on page 105, concealing seams.

HOW TO MAKE A CLOUD VALANCE FROM KITCHEN TOWELS

MATERIALS

- Kitchen towels; you will need enough towels to equal about two times the width of the rod, measuring towels lengthwise, because they will be turned sideways.
- 1" (2.5 cm) curtain rod with 2" (5 cm) projection.

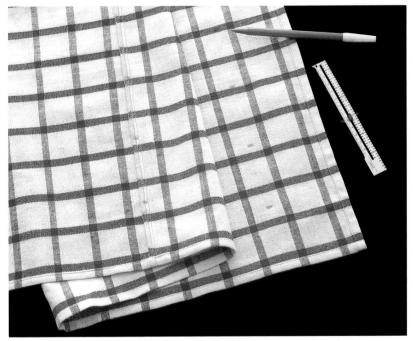

1 Seam towels together along short ends, right sides together. Fold under the upper edge of towels an amount equal to desired depth of heading and rod pocket; press. Stitch heading and rod pocket as on page 26, steps 3 and 4.

2 Mark pleat foldlines at each seam on wrong side of valance; measure up from lower edge, making four marks about 3½" (9 cm) apart. At sides of valance, mark pleat foldlines 3½" (9 cm) from ends of towels, spacing marks about 3½" (9 cm) apart.

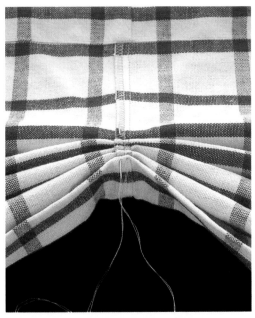

3 Fold lower edge up to meet first mark; then fold pleats in place, matching remaining marks. Tack pleats by hand, stitching close to folds through all layers.

4 Insert curtain rod through rod pocket, gathering fabric evenly. Install on brackets.

EASY SWAGS

For an instant window treatment, drape a single piece of fabric over a decorative pole or decorative hardware to create an informal swag with jabots, or side panels. The finished look can range from simple to elegant, casual to dramatic. Swags can be used alone to frame windows, or combined with curtains or blinds to embellish or soften the look.

For an easy, unlined swag without sewing, use the fabric yardage as it comes from the bolt, pressing back the selvages and fusing them in place. The hems of the jabots may be folded either diagonally or straight, then fused in place. Or the jabots can be puddled on the floor without hems, and bishop sleeves may be added, if desired.

For a finished look on the right and wrong sides, swags may be lined. It is especially desirable to line a swag if you want a contrasting color cascading down the inner edges of the jabots, or for more versatility in draping the fabric around the hardware.

Mediumweight decorator fabric, such as chintz and sateen, is recommended. Avoid heavyweight fabrics, which are bulky to work with and may not drape well. If using a patterned fabric, avoid fabric with a one-way design.

The key to beautiful swags is draping and arranging them. For a basic swag, drape the fabric over a decorative rod or hardware, and arrange the jabots as desired. For an asymmetrical look, the jabots may be different lengths, each draped differently.

After deciding on the placement of the hardware, decide what length you want the jabots to be; because the amount of fabric used for swags and jabots depends on the draping of the fabric at the window, you may want to avoid window treatments that require an exact finished length. Allow floor-length treatments to puddle on the floor, or plan for the length of the jabots to be about one-third or two-thirds the length of the window.

MATERIALS

- Decorator fabric.
- Lining fabric, for lined swag.
- Decorator pole set, tieback holders, or swag holders.
- Safety pins or double-stick tape, for securing fabric to pole or rod.
- Cording, for securing floor-puddled fabric.

CUTTING DIRECTIONS

Use the full width of the fabric. Determine the cut length of the panel by measuring the desired finished length of each jabot and the draped distance between the hardware brackets.

For an unlined swag, add 5" (12.5 cm) to this length for each jabot with a straight or diagonal hem; or add 18" to 26" (46 to 66 cm) for each jabot that will puddle on the floor and 15" (38 cm) for each bishop-sleeve jabot.

For a lined swag, add ½" (1.3 cm) seam allowance to this length for each jabot with a straight hem or diagonal hem; or add 18" to 26" (46 to 66 cm) for each jabot that will puddle on the floor and 15" (38 cm) for each bishop-sleeve jabot.

HOW TO MAKE AN UNLINED SWAG

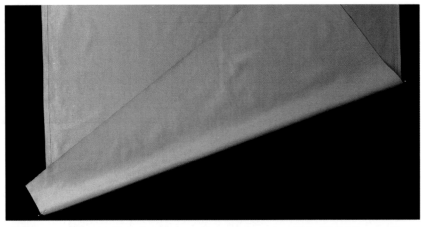

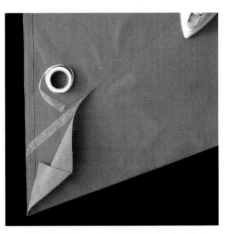

1 Diagonal hems. Press in selvages; fuse in place, to within 5" (12.5 cm) of outer corner of jabot. At both ends of fabric, pin-mark 5" (12.5 cm) from outer corner of jabot and 23" (58.5 cm) from inner corner. Fold fabric diagonally between pin marks; press.

2 Fold fabric even with fused side hems at outer corners; press. Fuse edges of jabot in place.

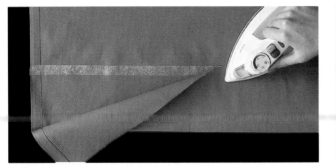

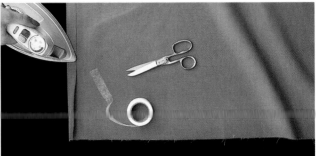

Straight hems. Press in selvages; fuse in place. Fold up 5" (12.5 cm) at lower edge; fuse in place.

Floor-puddled jabots. Press in selvages; fuse in place. Lower edge of fabric is left as a raw edge, which will be tucked under.

HOW TO MAKE A LINED SWAG

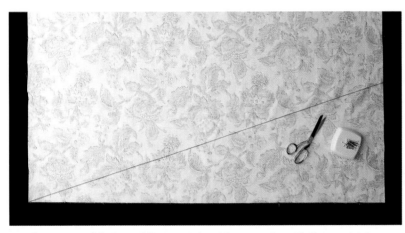

1 Place outer fabric and lining right sides together. If diagonal jabots are desired, pin-mark 18" (46 cm) from inner corners at both ends of fabric. Draw lines from pin marks diagonally to outer corner of fabric at opposite selvage. Cut on marked lines.

2 Stitch ½" (1.3 cm) seam around all four sides, leaving 12" (30.5 cm) opening at center of one long side for turning. Trim corners diagonally. Press seams open. Turn right side out; stitch opening closed. Press edges.

HOW TO DRAPE A SWAG

1 Drape the fabric over the pole or decorative hardware, placing fabric so jabots are at desired lengths. If jabots have diagonal hems, the shorter corners of the jabots will be toward the window.

2 Fan-fold fabric into generous pleats at each end where the panel drapes from the pole or hardware. Tug gently on the lower edge of the center swagged portion for desired drape; adjust folds.

3 Adjust folds in jabots. Secure fabric to top of pole or hardware with safety pins or double-stick tape, if necessary.

Bishop sleeves. Install swag holder about 6" (15 cm) higher than desired height for pouf of bishop sleeve. Insert fabric into swag holder. Arrange bishop sleeve, fanning and blousing fabric. Pin edges of fabric together in back to keep hardware from showing.

Floor-puddled jabots. Gather lower edge of fabric by hand if swag is unlined, and tie with cording, tucking raw edges inside; arrange fabric on floor as desired. If swag is lined, simply arrange fabric in soft folds, tucking under lower edge.

SWAG VARIATIONS

Knots tied in this lined panel hold the swag on the rod, creating a contemporary look. The fabric has been draped over the center of the rod to create two swags.

Brass towel rings serve as decorative hardware for this swag and coordinate with other brass accessories in the room.

Special decorative hardware, such as the Swags 'n Tails™ pole set (top), is designed especially for swags. On this pole set, the rings hold the swagged fabric in place, and the upper edge of the fabric is held taut to the back of the rod with self-adhesive hook and loop tape.

Ornate shelf brackets
are used as hardware
for this swag, and
decorative cording
with tassels is draped
with the fabric for
added detail.

Knotted jabots add
interest while they
secure the raw edges of
this unlined, no-sew
swag. Ribbons and
baby's breath are tied
around the knots for
an added touch.

DESIGNER WINDOW TREATMENTS

Top Treatments & Accessories

BASIC TOP
TREATMENTS

Rod-pocket valance *is used in conjunction with cafe curtains (page 28). Some privacy is provided, yet sunlight can filter into the room.*

Top treatments, used over curtains, draperies, or shades, give a custom look. They may also be used alone, to allow more light into the room and to frame a beautiful view. From the softly gathered or pleated valances to the more rigid cornices, there is a wide range of top treatment styles to choose from.

The basic styles of top treatments are usually just adaptations of curtains and draperies. Sewn in a shorter length, most styles of curtains and draperies can become valances. To make a valance, allow 4" (10 cm) for a 2" (5 cm) double-fold lower hem in the decorator fabric. If the valance will be lined, allow 2" (5 cm) for a 1"

(2.5 cm) double-fold hem in the lining. The cut length of the lining will be 3" (7.5 cm) shorter than the cut length of the decorator fabric.

There are very few rules for the use of top treatments. In general, the length of a top treatment should be in proportion to the total length of the window treatment. For valances, this length is usually about one-fifth of the window treatment, but cornices may be shorter to prevent them from appearing too overpowering or top-heavy. To add visual height to a room, a top treatment may be mounted several inches (centimeters) above the window or at the ceiling.

Arched rod-pocket valance *is a straight rod-pocket panel (page 25). Because an arched curtain rod is inserted into the rod pocket, the valance automatically becomes shaped.*

Valance with self-styling tape, *made like self-styling curtains (page 32), is installed on a pole set with rings.*

Pleated valance *is a variation of the pleated draperies with grouped pleats (page 44). Make one panel, allowing for a return on each side and no overlap. To keep the heading taut and even, the valance can be installed on a mounting board, using hook and loop tape, as on page 65, step 2. The valance and shutters are coordinated by using matching fabric for the shutter insets (page 117).*

Tie-tab valances *are made like tie-tab curtains (page 51). The valance, hung between two side panels, can be mounted on the same decorative rod.*

TAPERED VALANCES

Tapered valances frame the window with the graceful lines of a gentle curve. For a simple, no-fuss window treatment, they are often used with blinds or pleated shades. The valance cascades down the sides of the window, showing off the contrasting lining.

MATERIALS

• Decorator fabric.

• Lining fabric.

• Curtain rod or pole set.

CUTTING DIRECTIONS

Decide on the depth that will be used for the rod pocket and heading (page 25) at the top of the valance.

To determine the cut length of the valance, measure from the bottom of the rod to the desired length at the side; then add two times the depth of the rod pocket and heading plus 1" (2.5 cm) for seam allowance and turn-under. Cut the decorator fabric and lining to this length. Determine the cut width of valance and lining panels as for the rod-pocket curtain and lining panels on page 25.

To determine the cut length for the center portion of the valance, add two times the depth of the rod pocket and heading plus 1" (2.5 cm) for seam allowance and turn-under to the desired finished length at the center. This measurement is needed in step 1, below.

HOW TO SEW A TAPERED VALANCE

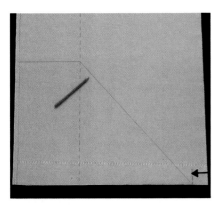

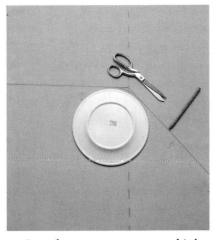

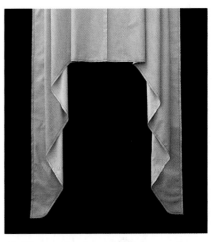

1 Seam fabric widths, if necessary. Divide and mark valance panel into thirds lengthwise, using chalk. Fold in half lengthwise; mark cut length for center portion from fold to one-third marking. Measure and mark depth of return at side (arrow). Draw a straight line from return mark to one-third marking at center length.

2 Round upper corner at one-third marking and lower corner at return. Pin fabric layers together; cut along marked lines, following markings for rounded corners. Cut lining panel, using valance panel as a pattern.

3 Place valance and lining panels right sides together. Stitch around side and lower edges in ½" (1.3 cm) seam, leaving upper edge open.

4 Press lining seam allowance toward lining. Clip seam allowances at curves, and trim corners at returns diagonally.

5 Turn valance right side out; press seamed edges. Press under ½" (1.3 cm) on upper edge, folding both layers as one; then press under an amount equal to rod-pocket depth plus heading depth. Stitch close to first fold. Stitch again at depth of heading, using tape on bed of machine as stitching guide.

6 Insert curtain rod through rod pocket, gathering fabric evenly. Install rod on brackets.

TAPERED
VALANCE
VARIATIONS

Ruffles *added to a tapered valance give a country flair. A wide curtain rod is used for this valance to emphasize the heading. For good proportion, the length of the valance is two-thirds the length of the window.*

Short tapered valances *keep the focal point of the window treatment at the top of the window. These shorter versions of the tapered valance may be unruffled (page 83), or ruffled (opposite).*

HOW TO SEW A RUFFLED TAPERED VALANCE

MATERIALS

- Decorator fabric.
- Lining fabric.
- Curtain rod or pole set.
- Cord, such as pearl cotton, for gathering.

CUTTING DIRECTIONS

Cut the valance and lining panels as on page 83. For the ruffle, cut fabric strips two times the finished width of the ruffle plus 1" (2.5 cm) for seam allowances. The combined length of the fabric strips is equal to two and one-half times the measurement along the curved edge of the valance.

1 Prepare valance and lining panels as on page 83, steps 1 and 2. Stitch fabric strips for ruffle together in ¼" (6 mm) seam, right sides together. Fold pieced strip in half lengthwise, right sides together; stitch across ends in ¼" (6 mm) seam. Turn right side out; press.

2 Zigzag over a cord within seam allowance of ruffle, just beyond seamline. Zigzag over a second cord ¼" (6 mm) from first cord, if desired, for more control when adjusting gathers.

3 Divide ruffle and curved edges of valance and lining panels into fourths or eighths; pin-mark, placing pins at sides of valance and lining panels ½" (1.3 cm) from raw edges. Place ruffle along curved edge of valance panel, right sides together, matching raw edges and pin marks; pull gathering threads to fit between pins. Machine-baste ruffle, leaving pin marks in place.

4 Place valance and lining panels right sides together, matching pin marks. Stitch around side and lower edges in ½" (1.3 cm) seam, leaving upper edge open. Finish the valance as on page 83, steps 4 to 6.

VALANCES FROM
TABLE LINENS

Table linens turn into beautiful valances quickly and easily by simply draping them and attaching them to a mounting board or cafe rod. You will need enough placemats, napkins, or tablecloths for the width of the treatment and the desired finished length.

For outside-mounted valances on a mounting board, determine how wide and deep the mounting board needs to be in order to clear the window frame or undertreatment. Cut the board and cover it with fabric, as on pages 16 and 17.

Bordered tablecloth *adds flair to a window. Fold the tablecloth on the diagonal and drape it over a cafe rod. Secure the tablecloth to the rod, using double-stick tape.*

MATERIALS

- Decorative placemats, napkins, table runners, or tablecloths, depending on style of valance; ribbons are also needed for some projects.
- Covered mounting board (page 16) or cafe rod and double-stick carpet tape, depending on style of valance.
- Angle irons, if treatment is to be mounted on mounting board; one angle iron for each end and one for every 45" (115 cm) interval across the width of the board.
- Heavy-duty stapler and staples.
- Pan-head screws or molly bolts (page 16).

Lace tablecloth *creates a soft valance. Stapled to a mounting board, this valance is tied gently with ribbon ties, as on page 89.*

Placemats *or napkins work well for valances (pages 88 and 89). When planning the placement of the linens, keep in mind that an odd number of points on the valance is visually more pleasing.*

Printed tablecloth *makes a simple swag for a small window. Center the table- cloth on a cafe rod, and secure one edge to the rod, using double-stick tape. Tie ribbon bows at the ends to create swag and jabots.*

CUTTING DIRECTIONS

Cut the mounting board and fabric, and cover the board (pages 16 and 17). The placemats are cut to fit after the placement is determined.

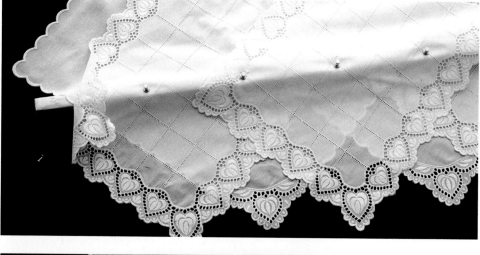

1 Arrange placemats, overlapping them to achieve a pleasing pattern. Check placement to make sure the arrangement is balanced. Tack the linens to the mounting board, using pushpins.

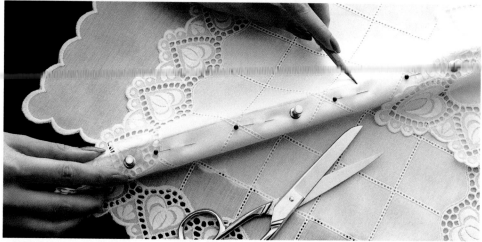

2 Pin linens together as overlapped. Draw a line on linens even with back edge of mounting board. Trim away excess fabric. Corners of placemats that have been trimmed away can be added to the valance as additional layers.

3 Remove valance from board, keeping linens pinned together. Stitch linens together; finish raw edges by serging or zigzagging.

4 Reposition linens on mounting board; staple in place. Mount valance as on page 17.

HOW TO MAKE A VALANCE FROM PLACEMATS (OUTSIDE MOUNT)

CUTTING DIRECTIONS

Cut the mounting board and fabric, and cover the board (pages 16 and 17). The placemats are cut to fit after the placement is determined.

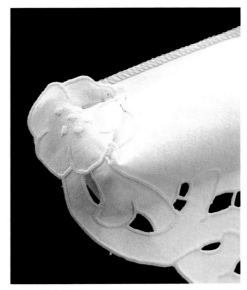

1 Arrange placemats, overlapping them to achieve a pleasing pattern and wrapping them around ends of mounting board. Check placement to make sure arrangement is balanced. Tack linens to mounting board, using pushpins.

2 Follow steps 2 to 4, opposite, mitering corners at ends.

HOW TO MAKE A VALANCE FROM A TABLECLOTH

CUTTING DIRECTIONS

Use a tablecloth the same width as, or wider than, the window to be covered; for outside-mounted valance, add returns to the width of the window. Cut the tablecloth at one end so the length of the valance is 14" to 18" (35.5 to 46 cm) longer than the desired finished length of the valance. Cut the mounting board and fabric, and cover the board (pages 16 and 17). Cut ribbons twice the desired finished length of the valance plus 4" (10 cm).

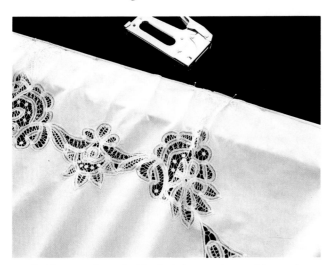

1 Finish raw edge of tablecloth by serging or zigzagging; staple edge to top of covered mounting board, centering tablecloth. Ease in excess fabric, if necessary, by making small tucks. For outside-mounted valance, wrap tablecloth around to sides of board, and miter corners, as shown above.

2 Position ribbon under valance at desired points; staple to boards. Pull ribbon around to the front of valance, and adjust to desired position; staple in place. Mount valance as on page 17.

CORNICES

A cornice is a wooden frame used as a top treatment. It not only frames and finishes a window treatment, hiding the hardware, but also saves energy by enclosing the top of the treatment.

This cornice is easy to build, requiring only simple carpentry skills. It is trimmed with decorative moldings, available in a variety of designs and sizes. Crown molding or chair rail frames the upper edge, and outside corner molding finishes the lower edge.

Cornices can be covered with wallpaper or lightly padded and covered with fabric. To avoid piecing, choose wallpaper or fabric that can be turned sideways and used lengthwise.

Take the measurements for the cornice after the drapery hardware is in place. The cornice should clear any undertreatment rod by at least 3" (7.5 cm), and it should extend at least 2" (5 cm) beyond the end brackets of the rod on each side. These measurements are the inside measurements of the cornice.

In determining the height of the cornice, keep in mind that the cornice should completely cover any drapery headings and hardware. Also the height of the cornice should be in proportion to the total length of the window or window treatment. A cornice may be up to one-fifth of the window treatment, but to keep the window treatment from appearing top-heavy or overpowering, smaller cornices are sometimes desired. Smaller cornices also look sleek, making them especially suitable for contemporary rooms.

MATERIALS

- ½" (1.3 cm) plywood.
- Outside corner molding, for the lower edge of the cornice; crown molding or chair rail, for the upper edge.
- Miter box and back saw, or power miter saw.
- Angle irons, shorter than the width of the board for the cornice top; flat-head wood screws.
- Wood glue; 16 × 1½" (3.8 cm) brads; heavy-duty stapler and staples.
- Paint; or stain and matching putty.
- Primer for unfinished wood, wallpaper, and wallpaper paste, for wallpapered cornice.
- Decorator fabric, lining, batting, spray adhesive, and fabric glue, for fabric-covered cornice.

CUTTING DIRECTIONS

Measure and cut the cornice top piece to correspond to the inside measurements, as calculated for clearance. Cut the cornice front piece to the desired height of the cornice; the cut width of the cornice front is equal to the width of the cornice top plus two times the thickness of the wood. Cut cornice side pieces to the height of the cornice by the depth of the cornice top.

The fabric, batting, wallpaper, and molding pieces are cut after step 2, below, based on the cornice measurements.

HOW TO MAKE A FABRIC-COVERED CORNICE

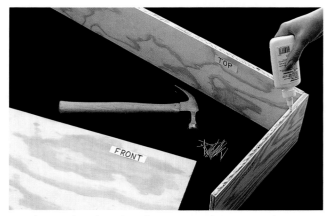

1 Glue and nail each side piece to top piece, aligning upper edges; secure with nails. Repeat for front piece, aligning it to top and side pieces.

2 Place corner molding on lower edge of cornice; mark a line on cornice front and sides at edge of molding. Repeat for crown molding or chair rail at the upper edge of the cornice.

(Continued)

3 Cut a strip of decorator fabric equal to height of cornice by the distance around the outside of the cornice plus 8" (20.5 cm); if necessary, fabric may be pieced and seamed together, pressing seams open. Cut batting equal to the distance between marked lines on cornice by the distance around cornice. Affix batting to the cornice between the marked lines, using spray adhesive, stretching the batting slightly across the width of the cornice.

4 Position fabric, right side up, centered on cornice front; secure with staples at center front, close to upper and lower edges. Pull fabric taut to one end of cornice; secure with staples on cornice side, near end. Repeat for opposite side.

5 Wrap fabric around the side piece to inside of cornice, mitering corner at upper edge; glue in place. Repeat for opposite side. Allow glue to dry; remove staples.

6 Glue raw edge of strip to cornice along lower edge; allow glue to dry. Smooth fabric taut to upper edge; glue in place.

7 Cut a piece of lining to inside height of cornice plus ½" (1.3 cm); length of lining is equal to inside measurement of front and sides. Secure lining to inside of cornice, using spray adhesive, aligning one long raw edge at the top. Clip lining at corners; glue to lower edges of boards. Cut a piece of lining to fit cornice top; affix, using spray adhesive.

8 Miter corner moldings for sides of cornice at front corners; leave excess length on the molding strips. Miter one corner on molding for the front of the cornice, leaving excess length.

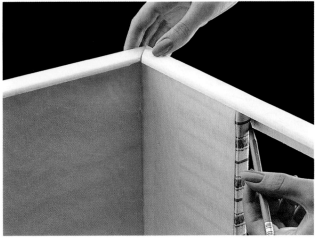

9 Position mitered front and side molding strips at one corner. Mark the finished length of the side piece for a straight-cut end.

10 Place side molding at opposite end. Using a straightedge, mark outside edge of front molding where miters will meet. Mark angle of cut. Cut miter.

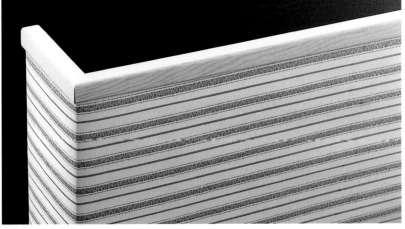

11 Reposition moldings; mark and straight-cut second side piece to fit.

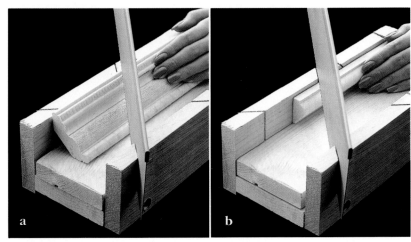

12 Cut crown molding or chair rail to fit around upper edge of cornice, following same sequence used for corner molding. To miter crown molding, place upper edge of molding tight against the bottom of miter box; cornice side should be tight against back of miter box **(a).** To miter the chair rail, place flat side of molding against back of miter box **(b).**

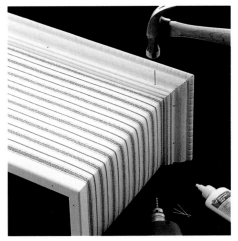

13 Paint or stain moldings as desired. Secure moldings to cornice, using finishing nails, predrilling nail holes with 1/16" (1.5 mm) drill bit. Use glue to secure mitered ends of moldings.

(Continued)

HOW TO MAKE A FABRIC-COVERED CORNICE (CONTINUED)

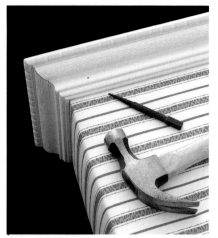

14 Secure upper edges of crown molding, if used, with one nail at each corner. Countersink nails, using a nail set; fill holes with putty to match stain, or touch up with paint.

15 Install cornice as for outside-mounted board on page 17; whenever possible, screw angle irons into wall studs instead of using molly bolts.

HOW TO MAKE A WALLPAPERED CORNICE

1 Follow step 1 on page 91; countersink nails on front of cornice at sides. Fill nail holes and side edges of cornice front board with wood filler; sand edges smooth.

2 Prime wood. Cut wallpaper equal to the height of the cornice by the distance around the outside of the cornice plus 8" (20.5 cm); wallpaper may be pieced by butting edges together, if necessary. Apply wallpaper, using wallpaper paste, wrapping ends around sides to inside of cornice.

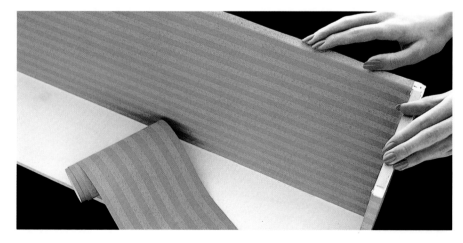

3 Cut a piece of wallpaper to inside height of cornice plus ½" (1.3 cm); length of wallpaper is equal to inside measurement of front and sides. Secure wallpaper to inside of cornice, using wallpaper paste, aligning one long edge to the top. Clip wallpaper at corners, and paste it to the lower edges of the cornice boards. Cut a piece of wallpaper to fit inside top of the cornice; apply with paste. Finish cornice as on pages 93 and 94, steps 8 to 15.

CORNICE VARIATIONS

Shaped wooden pieces *are covered with synthetic suede, then applied to the cornice for a dimensional effect.*

Plate rail *is applied to the top of a cornice for added interest. It is painted to match the molding.*

Picture framing *has been added to the front of a wallpapered cornice for architectural detailing.*

VENT HOSE CORNICES

Duplicate the look of designer hardware by using a vent hose, available at hardware stores. Cover the hose with fabric, and insert a curtain rod into the hose for a quick, contemporary cornice. A single covered hose may be used, or for a more substantial cornice, use two or three mounted next to each other.

For the cornice, use a curtain rod with a 5" (12.5 cm) projection. If the cornice is mounted over another window treatment, mount the undertreatment on a rod with a 2" (5 cm) projection. This allows for sufficient clearance between the undertreatment and the cornice; the vent hose itself takes up 1½" (3.8 cm) of the clearance between the rods. For clearance at the sides of an undertreatment, mount the curtain rod for the cornice 2" (5 cm) beyond the rod for the undertreatment. If the cornice is used alone, mount the cornice rod 2" (5 cm) beyond the window frame.

MATERIALS

- Decorator fabric.
- 3" (7.5 cm) flexible vinyl vent hose.
- Curtain rod with 5" (12.5 cm) projection.
- Masking tape or white tape.
- Two ½" (1.3 cm) cup hooks.

CUTTING DIRECTIONS

Stretch the vent hose slightly, and cut it to the length of the curtain rod, including returns; allow slack for going around the returns and for a loosely scrunched look. Cut a strip of fabric 11½" (29.3 cm) wide and two to three times the length of the rod; fabric strip may be pieced, if necessary.

HOW TO MAKE A CORNICE FROM VENT HOSE

1 Seam the fabric strips together as necessary. Fold strip in half lengthwise, right sides together; stitch ¼" (6 mm) seam. Turn right side out, and press. Wrap tape around ends of wire in vent hose. Slide fabric tube onto vent hose, leaving 1" (2.5 cm) of fabric extending beyond ends of hose; adjust fullness.

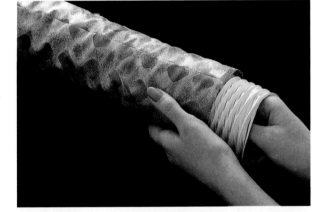

2 Fold ends of fabric tube to inside of the vent hose; hand-stitch in place, making sure to catch a row of wire. Insert curtain rod into the covered hose.

3 Install brackets (page 14), and mount rod. With top of covered hose resting on curtain rod, position hose against wall at return; mark wall lightly at side of hose.

4 Screw cup hook into the wall at mark. Secure covered hose on cup hook, puncturing vinyl; this holds hose flush against wall.

5 Form sharp corners, if desired, by compressing covered vent hose; glue fabric in place at corners, using hot glue.

TOP TREATMENTS AND ACCESSORIES

97

FLORAL TOP TREATMENTS

Create a custom floral top treatment to complement simple rod-pocket curtains or embellish an otherwise bare window. The floral arrangement serves as a cornice, creating an elegant look. The arrangement is attached to a thin wood strip, covered with paper ribbon. For an arch window, cut a 2" to 3" (5 to 7.5 cm) wood strip to the shape of the arch from ¼" (6 mm) plywood. The floral treatment may be attached to a curtain rod, using drapery hooks, or screwed into the wall at the sides of the window frame.

Design your own cornice, using moss, dried or silk flowers, silk greens, twigs, and ribbons. Or prepare the wood strip and have the arrangement made by a florist; bring fabric and paint swatches from your room to help the florist coordinate the arrangement.

Silk ivy *is the dominant item used for this wall-mounted top treatment; twigs and two kinds of silk ferns are also used. A wood strip cut to the shape of the arch-top window becomes the base for the floral items.*

A variety of silk flowers *is used for the rod-mounted top treatment shown at right. Silk greens, twigs, and wire ribbon are also strewn throughout the treatment.*

Bundles of straw *(opposite), bearded wheat, and other dried naturals are used for this wall-mounted treatment. Pheasant feathers and bittersweet berries are used as accents.*

- 2" (5 cm) wood strip, such as pine lattice, cut to length of curtain rod, for rod-mounted treatment; or 2" to 3" (5 to 7.5 cm) strip of ¼" (6 mm) plywood, cut to shape of window, for wall-mounted treatment.
- Paper twist, untwisted.
- Hot glue gun and glue sticks.
- Moss; dried flowers, silk flowers, silk greens, twigs, and ribbon, as desired.

- Floral wire, for arranging heavier objects.
- Curtain rod and drapery hooks to fit over curtain rod, for rod-mounted treatment; or 8 × 1" (2.5 cm) pan-head screws and plastic anchors, for wall-mounted treatment.
- Drill; 3/32" (2.38 mm) drill bit, for rod-mounted treatment; 5/32" (3.8 mm) drill bit, for wall-mounted treatment.

HOW TO MAKE A FLORAL TOP TREATMENT (MOUNTED ON ROD)

2 Predrill holes for drapery hooks; drill into edge of board, using 3/32" (2.38 mm) drill bit and placing holes at 10" to 12" (25.5 to 30.5 cm) intervals.

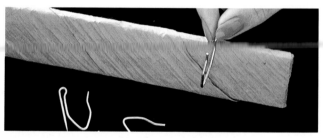

1 Wrap board with paper twist, securing it with hot glue.

3 Insert drapery hooks into drilled holes.

4 Secure layer of moss on front of board, if desired, using hot glue; moss conceals paper and provides background for design.

5 Arrange flowers, leaves, or other items as desired; for treatment shown here, start with background leaves, then add dominant flowers. Extend flowers, leaves, or other items beyond ends of board, for returns of curtain rod.

6 Complete the arrangement, filling in with additional leaves and flowers, as needed. Secure arranged flowers and leaves, using hot glue. Arrange ribbon as desired, forming loops; glue in place.

7 Hang cornice over curtain rod. For returns, attach moss to ends of curtain rod, using double-stick tape; glue or wire the flowers and leaves in place.

HOW TO MAKE A FLORAL TOP TREATMENT (MOUNTED ON WALL)

1 Follow step 1, opposite. Predrill holes for screws at ends and center of board, using 5/32" (3.8 mm) drill bit; additional screws may be needed for wider windows.

2 Follow steps 4, 5, and 6, opposite; do not extend flowers and leaves beyond ends of board in step 5.

3 Screw plywood into wall next to window frame, using plastic anchors (page 14).

TIEBACKS

Tieback curtains are a popular window fashion. Softly draped, these curtains are pulled to the sides, framing the window and letting in daylight. The tiebacks not only hold the curtain panels in place, but also add a finishing touch to the window treatment. They add color, texture, and interest to otherwise plain draperies.

The position of the tiebacks on the curtains affects the amount of exposed glass and the style of the treatment. Position tiebacks low to visually widen a window; position them high to visually add height. The most common positions are approximately one-third or two-thirds of the window height or, for floor-length window treatments, at the sill. If cafe curtains are used under the tieback curtains, the tiebacks are usually positioned at the level of the cafe rods.

Tiebacks are generally used for stationary curtain panels, because the panels need to be arranged, or dressed, into even folds. For a professional-looking installation, use concealed tieback holders (page 13) under the curtain panels at the height of the tiebacks; the tieback holders project out from the wall an amount equal to the return of the curtains, to prevent crushing the folds of the window treatment.

Tailored tiebacks (page 104) are easy to sew and simple in styling. These basic tiebacks can be made from a coordinating fabric.

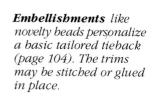

Embellishments like novelty beads personalize a basic tailored tieback (page 104). The trims may be stitched or glued in place.

Garlands, *used as tiebacks, frame a scenic view. Wire the ends of the garlands to tenter hooks mounted on the wall.*

Tasseled tiebacks *(page 104) are two-piece tiebacks knotted like a man's necktie.*

Braided tiebacks *(page 105), made from decorative cording, add texture and interest to tailored tiebacks.*

Ruching *and other creative trims can be draped and tied in unconventional ways.*

Trimmings, *such as twisted cording with tassels, work well as tiebacks. One curtain panel is pulled to the center of the window for a unique look.*

HOW TO MAKE A TAILORED TIEBACK

MATERIALS

- Mediumweight decorator fabric.
- Fusible interfacing.
- Tieback rings, two for each tieback.

CUTTING DIRECTIONS

Determine the finished length of tiebacks by measuring around curtain at desired tieback location. Cut one piece of decorator fabric for each tieback, the finished length plus 1" (2.5 cm) and two times the desired finished width plus 1" (2.5 cm). Cut one piece of interfacing for each tieback, the finished length and width of tieback.

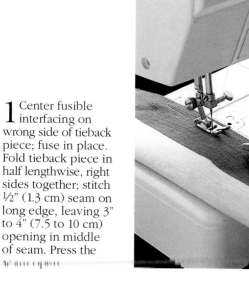

1 Center fusible interfacing on wrong side of tieback piece; fuse in place. Fold tieback piece in half lengthwise, right sides together; stitch ½" (1.3 cm) seam on long edge, leaving 3" to 4" (7.5 to 10 cm) opening in middle of seam. Press the seam open.

2 Center seam on back of tieback; stitch across short ends in ½" (1.3 cm) seams. Trim corners diagonally; trim seam allowances at short ends to ¼" (6 mm).

3 Turn tieback right side out through opening. Slipstitch opening closed. Secure tieback rings to wrong side of tieback, with one ring centered near each end.

HOW TO MAKE A TASSELED TIEBACK

MATERIALS

- Decorator fabric.
- Lightweight fusible interfacing.
- Small tassels, two for each tieback.
- Tieback rings, two for each tieback.

CUTTING DIRECTIONS

Measure around curtain at desired tieback location to determine the length needed to wrap around curtain panel. Cut four 3" (7.5 cm) fabric strips for each tieback, with each strip one-half the measured length plus 20" (51 cm) for the knot and tail. Cut two strips of lightweight fusible interfacing for each tieback, to same size as fabric strips.

1 Center fusible interfacing on wrong side of tieback piece; fuse in place. Mark sides of tieback 3" (7.5 cm) from one end. Cut end of tieback to a point, cutting from marks to bottom center. At other end, press under ½" (1.3 cm).

2 Stitch two strips, right sides together, in ½" (1.3 cm) seam. Stitch sides and tapered end of tieback, leaving ¼" (6 mm) unstitched at point. Trim tapered end, being careful not to trim too close at point.

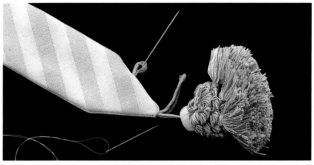

3 Turn tieback right side out; press. Insert tassel cord into opening at tapered end, using large-eyed needle; hand-stitch to secure. Slipstitch remaining end closed.

4 Make two finished tieback pieces for each tieback. Attach tieback rings to wrong side of each tieback piece, centering ring near the end. After securing the tiebacks (below), knot tieback pieces together as for man's necktie.

HOW TO MAKE A BRAIDED TIEBACK

MATERIALS

- Decorator fabric.
- Fusible interfacing.
- Decorative cording.
- Tieback rings, two for each tieback.

CUTTING DIRECTIONS

Determine the finished length of tiebacks by measuring around curtain at desired tieback location. Cut decorator fabric and interfacing as for tailored tieback, opposite. Cut four pieces of decorative cording two times the finished length of tieback.

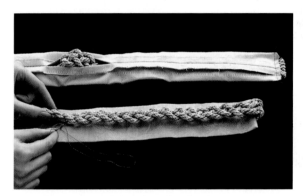

1 Stitch cords together at one end, butting them tightly; pin to padded surface, spreading cords flat. Braid cord at far right to the left, braiding over first cord, under second cord, and over third cord.

2 Braid the next cord at far right, repeating over, under, and over motion. Continue in this manner until braid is about 2" (5 cm) longer than tieback. Stitch end as in step 1.

3 Follow step 1 for tailored tieback, opposite. Center seam on back of tieback; insert braid into tieback. Center braid at each short end; matching raw edges, stitch across ends in ½" (1.3 cm) seams. Trim corners diagonally; trim seam allowances to ¼" (6 mm). Finish tieback as in step 3, opposite. Tack braid in place.

SECURING THE TIEBACKS

1 Secure inner end of tieback onto hook on concealed tieback holder. Run your fingers down the fold of each pleat, adjusting curtain panel into position; start at outer side.

2 Secure outer end onto outside of tieback holder. Adjust position of tieback, continuing to fold panel below tieback to lower edge of curtain.

DECORATIVE
POLE SETS

A decorative pole set adds the finishing touch to a window treatment. Unfinished poles, finials, and rings can be transformed into custom hardware by sponging them with paint, pickling them with colored stains, or covering them with fabric.

Unfinished poles, finials, and rings *are available in many styles.*

1) Fabric-covered ball finials and pole *(pages 108 and 109) can be customized to coordinate with other fabrics and trims in the room.*

2) Hand-painted pineapple finials and pole *are elegantly gilded with gold metallic paint.*

3) Sponged wood pole set *(page 108) is painted, using natural sea sponges. The paint is dabbed onto the wood, creating a mottled, irregular appearance.*

4) Rosebud finials *(pages 110 and 111) and fabric-covered pole (pages 108 and 109) soften the look of traditional wooden hardware.*

5) Pickled wood pole set with rings *is finished using a colored stain, available from a paint-supply store. Follow the manufacturer's instructions for applying the stain.*

5

HOW TO SPONGE WOOD POLES, FINIALS & RINGS

MATERIALS

- Natural sea sponges; use 2" (5 cm) pieces of sponge.
- Primer for unfinished wood.
- Paint in desired background color for base coat and one or two accent colors.
- Styrofoam® block, for supporting wooden rings and finials while drying.
- Newsprint, for blotting excess paint.

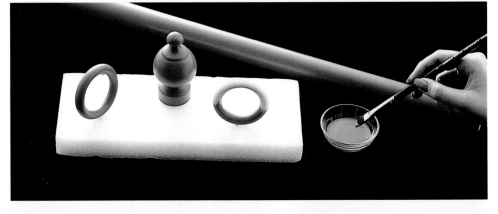

1 Apply the primer to the unfinished wood. Apply base coat in desired background color; allow to dry. Push eye of ring or screw of finial into block of Styrofoam to support them while drying.

2 Rinse sponge in water to soften it; squeeze dry. Dab sponge into accent-color paint, taking care not to overload it. Blot sponge on newsprint until you get a light impression. Press sponge gently onto surface, using light touch; repeat throughout entire project. Change position of sponge frequently for irregular impressions, and apply more paint to sponge, as necessary. Rinse sponge; allow paint to dry.

3 Repeat sponging with second accent color.

HOW TO MAKE A FABRIC-COVERED POLE

MATERIALS

- Decorator fabric.
- Wood pole.
- Mounting brackets designed to be used with Cirmosa® rods.
- Fabric glue.
- Tacks; or heavy-duty stapler and staples.

CUTTING DIRECTIONS

For 1⅜" (3.5 cm) diameter wood poles, cut the decorator fabric to the rod circumference plus 1½" (3.8 cm) by the length of the pole. Or for 2" (5 cm) diameter wood poles, cut the fabric to the rod circumference plus 1¾" (4.5 cm) by the length of the pole.

1 Hold pole firmly against table; using pencil placed flat on table, draw line on pole.

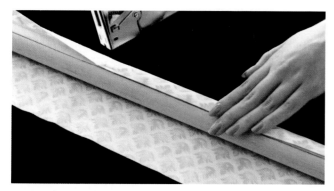

2 Staple or tack one edge of fabric to pole, aligning raw edge with marked line.

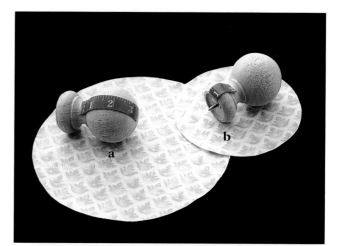

3 Wrap fabric snugly around pole. Fold under raw edge; staple or tack in place. Apply glue around end of pole; adhere fabric. Allow glue to dry.

HOW TO MAKE A FABRIC-COVERED BALL FINIAL

MATERIALS

- Ball finials to fit diameter of wood pole.
- Decorator fabric.
- Cord, braid, or other trim.
- Fabric glue; two rubber bands for each finial.

CUTTING DIRECTIONS

Measure ball portion of finial from top of finial to neck **(a)**; cut one fabric circle for each finial, with radius 1" (2.5 cm) longer than measurement.

Measure crown portion of finial from neck to base **(b)**; cut one fabric circle for each finial, with radius 1" (2.5 cm) longer than measurement.

1 Center the ball of the finial on fabric circle for ball portion; wrap fabric around ball to neck of finial. Secure fabric at neck with rubber band, adjusting fullness evenly; trim fabric to within ½" (1.3 cm) of rubber band.

2 Pierce center of fabric circle for crown portion; twist fabric over the screw. Attach finial to the wood pole.

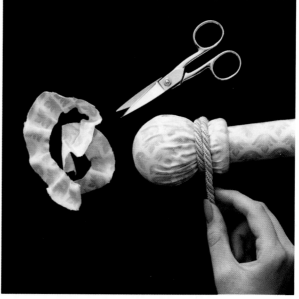

3 Apply glue around neck of finial. Wrap fabric circle around neck, securing with second rubber band and adjusting gathers evenly; allow glue to dry. Trim fabric next to rubber band. Cover rubber band with cord, braid, or other trim.

HOW TO MAKE A ROSEBUD FINIAL

MATERIALS

- Decorative finials to fit 1⅜" (3.5 cm) wood pole.
- Decorator fabric.
- Polyurethane foam, ¼" (6 mm) thick.
- Fabric glue.
- Self-adhesive hook and loop tape.

CUTTING DIRECTIONS

For a pair of finials, cut one 10½" (26.8 cm) square and two 12" × 15" (30.5 × 38 cm) rectangles from decorator fabric; also cut two 3" × 10" (7.5 × 25.5 cm) fabric strips from decorator fabric, with one long edge along selvage. Cut one 10½" (25.3 cm) square of foam.

Fold squares of fabric and foam in half diagonally; cut along fold, making two triangles of each.

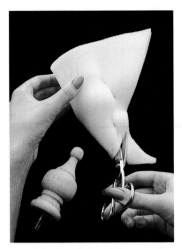

1 Wrap triangle of foam around finial; pin in place. Trim sides to shape of finial.

2 Stitch side edges of foam together. Trim foam even with lower edge of finial.

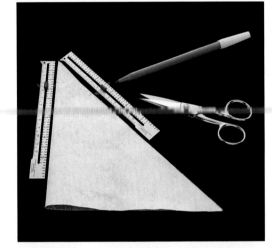

3 Fold triangle of fabric in half, matching raw edges. Mark foldline 1¼" (3.2 cm) from corner with 45° angle. Mark raw edge 2½" (6.5 cm) from same corner. Draw curved line, connecting marks; trim along marked line.

4 Stitch ¼" (6 mm) seam along curved edge; trim to ⅛" (3 mm).

5 Turn the rosebud right side out; fit over finial, pulling fabric tight over foam. Adjust seamline by restitching, if necessary, for smooth fit. Trim lower edge of fabric so the raw edge extends 1" (2.5 cm) beyond finial.

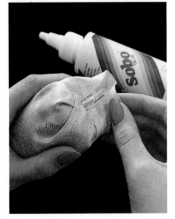

6 Fold lower edge of fabric to the bottom of the finial, adjusting gathers evenly; secure, using fabric glue.

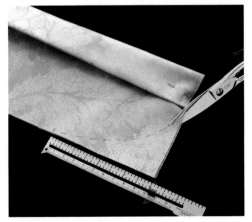

7 Fold 12" × 15" (30.5 × 38 cm) rectangle in half lengthwise; press lightly. Bring folded edge over 1½" (3.8 cm); pin in place at ends, but do not press. On lower edge, measure 4" (10 cm) from short ends; mark. At sides, draw curved line from mark to folded edge; trim along marked line.

8 Stitch two rows of gathering stitches along curve, within ⅜" (1 cm) seam allowances. Gather petal to measure about 5½" (14 cm).

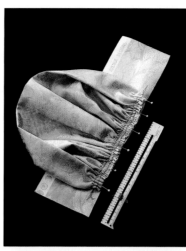

9 Place the petal, with folded side facing up, on right side of 3" × 10" (7.5 × 25.5 cm) fabric strip, with petal 1½" (3.8 cm) from one short end of strip and raw edges even. Stitch ⅜" (1 cm) seam.

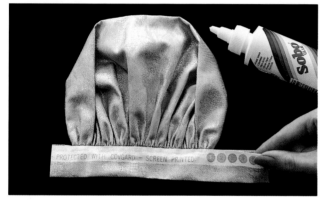

10 Press seam allowance toward fabric strip. Fold in short ends ½" (1.3 cm); press. Fold strip lengthwise, with wrong sides together and selvage just below folded upper edge. Secure edges, using fabric glue.

11 Position hook side of hook and loop tape on side of fabric strip with selvage, centered near one edge. Screw finial onto covered pole. Wrap petal and fabric strip around rosebud; position loop side of tape on fabric strip, aligned under hook side of tape.

12 Adjust finial so seam of rosebud is at back of pole. Wrap petal around pole; overlap of fabric strip will be in back of pole.

INSTALLING A DECORATIVE POLE WITH FINIALS

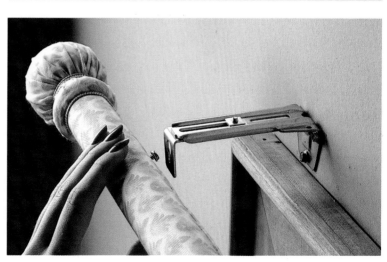

Attach brackets to wall or window frame, using molly bolts or pan-head screws (page 14). Attach screws to covered pole, positioning them the same distance apart as keyhole openings on brackets. Hang covered pole on brackets.

Alternative
Window
Treatments

SHELVES

Shelves may be hung above windows as novelty top treatments. Mounted in front of a window, they can be used to showcase plants and collections. Shelves can be used alone or in combination with other window treatments.

Decorative shelves and brackets are available in a variety of styles, including glass, laminates, and hardwood boards. Follow the manufacturer's instructions for mounting the shelf brackets, mounting them either on the window frame or the wall.

For customized shelving, finish wooden shelves with stain or paint that matches the woodwork of the window. Or add hooks or dowels to the shelves.

Stained wooden shelf (above) has been mounted above the window, with the brackets positioned on the wall next to the window frame. Baskets hang below the wooden shelf for an eclectic look. For this treatment, attach large hooks to the bottom of the shelf.

Glass shelves are used to display a collection of decorative bottles. Cut the shelves to recess into the window, if desired.

Painted shelf *is mounted above a valance with self-styling tape (page 81). Cut the shelf to the depth of the curtain rod projection, and mount the shelf brackets so they are concealed under the valance.*

Wood pole *can be used for hanging dried flowers and herbs or as a curtain rod. Drill holes into the sides of wooden shelf brackets and insert a wood pole or dowel through the holes.*

SHUTTERS

Wooden shutters have long been a popular window treatment, adding charm to any window setting. Accordion-fold shutters may be used on almost any window, including sliding glass doors. They offer privacy and open neatly to expose the full width of the window. Shutters with louvers offer greater light control than many window treatments.

To ensure that they fit properly, custom shutters, measured and installed by a professional, are recommended. Order the shutters unfinished if you want to paint or stain them to coordinate with your decor.

For an interesting look, paint the shutters or "pickle" them with a colored stain. Instead of matching the window frame, the shutters may be finished to match one of the fabrics in the room.

Nonfunctional shutters *(opposite) serve as decorative side panels. These shutters have been stained with colored stain, following the manufacturer's instructions.*

Painted shutters *coordinate with fabrics in the room.*

Accordion-fold shutters *can be used for sliding glass doors, to provide privacy.*

Insets in shutters *can be either stretched rod-pocket panels or wallpaper insets. For rod-pocket panels, install the panels using small rods mounted behind the shutter; allow for narrow side hems and ½" (1.3 cm) headings, which prevent a light gap at the top and bottom. For wallpaper insets, apply the wallpaper to heavy cardboard, cut larger than the opening in the frame of the shutters; staple the covered cardboard to the back of the shutters.*

FAUX STAINED GLASS

Simulate traditional stained glass by using a specialty paint designed for this purpose. The designs are outlined with a simulated liquid leading and then filled in with the stained glass paint. Embellish an entire window with faux stained glass or frame a window with a border design. For a unified look, apply related borders to windows of different sizes and shapes.

This technique is for indoor use only and is not intended for windows in areas with excessive humidity. Do not apply stained glass paints to windows where moisture condenses. Stained glass designs can be removed by loosening an edge with a mat knife and peeling the entire project from the glass.

For the design motifs, use the pattern sheets intended for stained glass or design your own motifs, using cutwork patterns or art books for ideas. Patterns can be custom-sized to the window by enlarging designs on a photocopy machine or by varying the size of the borders.

Avoid the use of self-adhesive lead strips, which can be easily removed by children and are toxic. The simulated liquid leading in the instructions that follow does not contain lead.

Because it is easier to work on glass placed on a work table, remove the window, if possible. The project can be done vertically if necessary. Refer to the manufacturer's instructions for the climate conditions recommended for application.

MATERIALS

- Stained glass paint and simulated liquid leading, available from craft and hobby stores.
- Smudgeproof carbon paper or graphite paper.
- Masking tape; toothpicks; lint-free cloth.
- Plastic wrap.

TIPS FOR MAKING FAUX STAINED GLASS

Clean and dry the window thoroughly before you apply the liquid leading. Remove any dirt, grease, or fingerprints, using a lint-free cloth.

Select a simple design for your first project. It is more difficult to apply simulated liquid leading to small, intricate design areas.

Apply darker colors to smaller design sections for better coverage. Or apply a second coat of paint, if necessary.

Mix stained glass paints together to achieve a wider range of colors.

Test the colors you plan to use, and practice the technique before starting a large project.

Recessed window becomes a spectacular focal point with faux stained glass.

Faux stained glass is easy to create following the steps on pages 120 and 121. Simulated liquid leading is applied to the glass first. Then the stained glass paint is applied to fill in the design areas. The paint becomes clear and sparkles when dry.

HOW TO MAKE FAUX STAINED GLASS (HORIZONTAL METHOD)

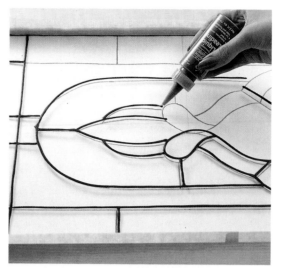

1 Cover work area; protect edges of woodwork with masking tape. Place pattern under glass, taping in place.

2 Squeeze bottle of liquid leading with even pressure and, keeping tip of bottle above surface of glass, apply a cord of leading onto glass along design lines. Stop squeezing bottle near the end of design line, and lower tip to surface at end.

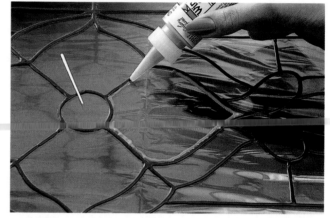

3 Allow at least 8 hours for leading to dry. When dry, irregularities can be trimmed off, using a mat knife; reapply leading as necessary.

4 Apply paint to glass directly from tubes, starting by outlining design areas. Make sure paint is sealed up to edge of leading to prevent light gaps; use toothpick as necessary to fill corners and edges. (Paint appears milky when wet.)

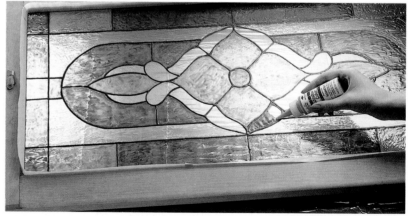

5 Continue to apply paint within section of design, working back and forth; use toothpick to help distribute paint and remove bubbles. A few bubbles may remain to give a more authentic look.

6 Apply the paint to remaining sections. Allow paint to dry, following manufacturer's recommendations for drying time. Additional coats may be applied to intensify colors. Allow at least one week for project to cure before cleaning. Faux stained glass may then be cleaned by wiping it lightly with a soft cloth.

1 Mark lines on a sheet of legal-size paper; place on a piece of cardboard, and cover with a sheet of plastic wrap. Apply liquid leading as in step 2, opposite, following lines on paper. Allow at least 72 hours for leading to dry.

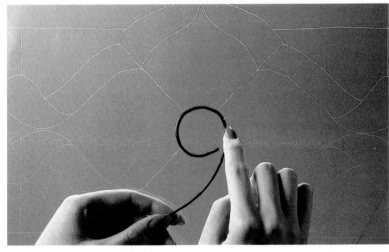

2 Protect woodwork with masking tape and newspaper. Transfer pattern, using graphite paper; or tape pattern in place on outside of glass. Trim any irregularities from leading. Peel leading strips from plastic and apply to glass, following design lines; do not stretch strips.

3 Piece leading strips as necessary. Trim intersecting lines with mat knife so strips meet; do not overlap.

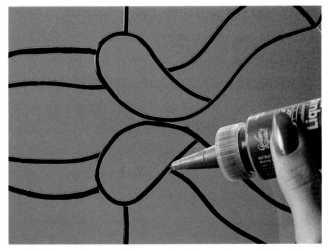

4 Fill in any spaces between leading strips, and touch up, if necessary, using liquid leading. Allow to dry at least 8 hours before applying paint.

5 Apply paint, following steps 4 to 6, opposite, working from top to bottom; take care that paint does not run.

ETCHED GLASS

Customize your windows with etching for a charming embellishment. A subtle design can draw attention to a beautiful view or enhance a special molding. Etching may be the only window treatment that is used on some windows. Depending on the design used for the etching, the effect can be turn-of-the-century or contemporary.

The etching cream, available from craft stores, is applied over a stencil to create the etched glass. You may make your own custom stencil, cut from self-adhesive vinyl; designs intended for stained glass and cutwork work well for cutting your own stencils. Or you may use precut etching stencils, also available from craft stores. If precut stencils are used, apply the stencil and etch the glass according to manufacturer's instructions. The amount of time the etching cream remains on the glass varies with the type of stencil.

For best results, use a simple design with small areas for etching; large, solid areas of glass may become blotchy in appearance. To become familiar with the technique, practice on a scrap of glass before etching the window.

Etching may be done on either the inside or outside of the window. Because it is easier to work on glass placed on a work table, remove the glass or the window, if possible. Etching can be done vertically if the glass or window is not removable.

Before you apply the stencil, clean and dry the window thoroughly, using a lint-free cloth, removing any dirt, grease, or fingerprints. Also plan how you will rinse the project. Mask off any areas on the woodwork or walls that could come in contact with the rinse water, as well as any areas on the glass that are not protected by the stencil. If you are working on the window vertically, tape a plastic drop cloth to the window below the design area to be etched. Place the drop cloth in a large pail, and allow the rinse water to flow down the drop cloth into the bucket.

MATERIALS

- Precut stencils or self-adhesive vinyl, such as Con-Tact®, and mat knife.
- Etching cream; soft-bristle brush.
- Smudgeproof carbon paper or graphite paper.
- Masking tape; plastic drop cloth.
- Lint-free cloths; rubber gloves.

Etched border design *decorates a window without obstructing the view.*

Etched grid design, *interrupted with floral motifs, gives this awning window a frosted effect.*

Etched motifs *(opposite) embellish arched French doors for an elegant exit to the patio.*

HOW TO APPLY A PRECUT ETCHING STENCIL

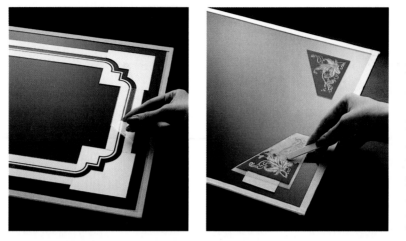

Adhesive stencil. Separate stencil from backing sheet and position with adhesive side touching the glass. Allow 5 to 10 minutes for adhesive to bond. Remove top sheet, and follow steps 4 and 5, below.

Rub-off stencil. Secure the stencil temporarily with masking tape. Rub entire stencil firmly but gently, using a wooden stick, to transfer stencil to glass. Remove the top sheet carefully, checking to see that stencil is completely adhered.

HOW TO MAKE & APPLY A CUSTOM STENCIL

1 Cut self-adhesive vinyl 2" (5 cm) larger than design. Remove the paper backing, and affix vinyl to window, pressing out any air bubbles. If more than one width of vinyl is needed, overlap edges ½" (1.3 cm). Allow 5 to 10 minutes for adhesive to bond securely.

2 Position design on window, with carbon or graphite paper under design; tape in place. Trace design onto vinyl.

3 Cut around design areas to be etched, using mat knife, applying just enough pressure to cut through vinyl. At corners, do not cut past the point of intersecting lines.

4 Remove vinyl in design areas to be etched, using tip of knife blade to loosen edge of vinyl.

5 Press firmly on all cut edges of vinyl, using lint-free cloth.

HOW TO ETCH THE WINDOW GLASS

1 Cover woodwork, walls, or any areas of the glass not protected by the stencil with masking tape or plastic drop cloth.

2 Apply a thick layer of etching cream over entire design area, wearing rubber gloves and using soft-bristle brush. For custom stencils, allow etching cream to remain on design 6 to 10 minutes; for precut stencils, follow manufacturer's instructions. While cream is reacting, gently move cream with brush to make sure there are no air bubbles or uncovered areas.

3 Rinse design thoroughly to remove all etching cream, working from top to bottom; use brush to aid in removal of cream, being careful not to tear stencil. Do not allow rinse water to come in contact with woodwork or walls.

4 Pat area dry, using lint-free cloth. Remove stencil.

INDEX

CREDITS

CY DECOSSE INCORPORATED
Chairman: Cy DeCosse
President: James B. Maus
Executive Vice President:
  William B. Jones

CREATIVE WINDOW TREATMENTS
Created by: The Editors of
  Cy DeCosse Incorporated.

Also available from the publisher:
*Bedroom Decorating, Decorating
for Christmas*

Executive Editor: Zoe A. Graul
Technical Director: Rita C. Opseth
Project Manager: Linda Halls
Senior Art Director: Lisa Rosenthal
Writer: Rita C. Opseth
Editors: Janice Cauley, Bernice Maehren
Sample Coordinator: Carol Olson
Technical Photo Director: Bridget Haugh
Photo Stylists: Patrice Dingmann,
  Coralie Sathre

Styling Director: Bobbette Destiche
Fabric Editor: Joanne Wawra
Research Assistant: Lori Ritter
Sewing Staff: Phyllis Galbraith, Bridget
  Haugh, Sara Macdonald, Linda
  Neubauer, Carol Olson, Carol Pilot,
  Nancy Sundeen
*Director of Development Planning
  & Production:* Jim Bindas
Photo Studio Managers: Cathleen
  Shannon, Rena Tassone
Lead Photographers: John Lauenstein,
  Mette Nielsen
Photographers: Rex Irmen, Mark
  Macemon, Paul Najlis, Mike Parker,
  Dave Brus, Chuck Neilds, Marc
  Scholtes
Production Manager: Amelia Merz
Production Staff: Adam Esco, Joe Fahey,
  Peter Gloege, Melissa Grabanski, Eva
  Hanson, Jeff Hickman, Paul Najlis,
  Mike Schauer, Linda Schloegel, Nik
  Wogstad
Prop & Rigging Supervisor: Greg Wallace
Scenic Carpenters: Tom Cooper, Jim
  Huntley, Wayne Wendland

Consultants: Pamela Damour, Joyce
  Eide, Kathy Ellingson, Amy Engman,
  Roseann Fairchild, Wendy Fedie,
  Maureen Klein, Donna Whitman
Contributors: Armour Products; Coats &
  Clark Inc.; Conso Products Company;
  Dritz Corporation; Dyno Merchandise
  Corporation; Gosling Tapes; Graber
  Industries, Inc.; Kirsch; Marvin Windows,
  Inc.; Murtra Industries, U.S.A.; Sheridan;
  The Singer Company; Swiss-Metrosene,
  Inc.; Waverly, Division of F. Schumacher
  & Company
Printed on American paper by: Ringier
  America, Inc. (0992)

Cy DeCosse Incorporated offers
craft and sewing accessories to
subscribers. For information write:
  Craft Accessories
  5900 Green Oak Drive
  Minnetonka, MN 55343